LITTLE CABIN ON THE TRAIL

LITTLE CABIN ON THE TRAIL

~an unofficial handbook of sorts

DENISE MAHR VOCCOLA

For Grandma and Nate.
Because of your love.
Because of your courage.
Because of your stories.
Because you both taught
me so much about life.

Contents

Hello There 9

Stories 13

Characters 23

Clever.. 35

Holidays & Traditions............................... 43

Happenstance 53

Family Fodder.. 67

Simple Things 81

Extreme Faith... 95

The Cabin... 107

Words.. 117

Treasure... 139

Much Love & Big Thanks 151

Hello There

Memory is the diary that we all carry about with us.
—OSCAR WILDE

In 2000. I penned a book that I entitled *Grandma*, because it was about—yes, you guessed it—my grandma. It wasn't published. It wasn't that kind of book. I wrote it as a gift for my brother and sister. It honored a woman who, although extremely poor, left behind a rich legacy of memories for her grandchildren. I detailed everything from our childhood that I could remember about the amazing grandmother who loved us unconditionally. I included things that she and I did together and things she taught me. I wrote about what she wore and how she spent her days. I revisited the places we went. By today's standards, all of the experiences that make up my fondest childhood memories would not appear to be very impressive, yet they continue to bring me joy and give me a sense of well-being.

There were no trips to Disney World or the beach. We did, however, frequently walk the steep hills of

Pittsburgh to go to the grocery store and "baker shop." And sometimes we'd walk to church to light a candle for my dad. Her affirmation of me did not come through gifts, although I was given a precious dollar for good report card grades. It came through spending time doing the simplest things, like playing cards and sitting on the front porch in the evening. It came through making "meatball stew" together and washing and drying dishes together after dinner.

I have always known that I had a book inside me. Up until now, I have never had the courage, discipline, direction, or whatever it took to actually pen one. While praying a few years ago, I felt impressed to consider what I wanted the last leg of my journey here on earth to look like. I contemplated what I would regret not doing before I died. I guess you could say that I reviewed my bucket list and had a reality check. At age 55, skydiving was easy to scratch off, but writing a book was not. So I began to specifically pray that the Lord would give something worthwhile to me to write about, and I believe He answered that prayer.

Little did I know then that just 15 days after hearing the call to write about memories, mine would be violently attacked through the tragic deaths of my grandson, Nate, and his friend, Noah. Both boys were electrocuted on the 4th of July while swimming off the side of our houseboat—a place where we had made many memories together. In a split second, our world came crashing down as we helplessly watched two young boys leave this world for another.

In the days and weeks to follow, my family and I

first faced the pain of memories and then the comfort of memories. We evaluated choices we had made—to embrace the simpler things of life, to live together with intentionality, to create moments worth remembering. In the end, we found that our choices left us with no regrets. Our time with Nate was short, but that time was well spent.

Stories

The business of life is the acquisition of memories.
—MR. CARSON, *DOWNTON ABBEY*

Our lives are but a story in this book called life. Wow, that sounded so philosophical and canned—and who-cares-boring. Let me try that again. Your life experiences and my life experiences are so incredibly fascinating that they must be shared. That's right—they must be shared. At this point, whether you believe it or not does not change the fact that it is true. This book is chock-full of unscientifically proven facts that you will just need to accept. We can review my credentials later.

I have always been an intentional memory-maker and a natural storyteller. Nothing is more satisfying to me than a captive audience. It doesn't matter if it is an audience of one or one hundred. I am actually happy to tell a good story to myself. To be able to engage others through storytelling is powerful. Words are powerful. The Bible tells us that life and death are in the power of the tongue. Think about that. We have the potential to bring forth life through our words or death through our words. We have the potential to bring forth life through our stories.

Stories are most often birthed in our life experiences. Those experiences filter through our perspective filters and our belief systems to be categorized and deposited into our memory banks to be withdrawn as needed. While we may not be given carte blanche on the big scripts of our lives, we are given plenty of creative license when it comes to the stories within the *story*.

At this stage in my life, I realize more than ever before the important role that meaningful memories play in the well-being of my family and in all families for that matter. I am not talking about the kind of memories that are being made on the hamster wheel of life as we now know it. I am talking about the memories that give us stories to pass down, stories to tell around the holiday table, stories that insist on being retold again and again.

I have found that those stories are most often birthed in the ordinary moments on the ordinary days, not as a result of well-laid plans or elaborately orchestrated events. More often than not, my family's best memories are about experiences that happened when we least expected them to—when we seized the moments and capitalized on the opportunities that presented before us.

I have a two-fold reason for writing this book. The first is to preserve and the second is to encourage. My stories are my stories and they are meaningful to me and my family. I want them recorded so that we never forget what made us laugh and what made us cry and what made us unique. I also want to encourage everyone else to assign value to what made their families laugh and cry and stand out from the crowd.

Our family has been known to spend the Friday after Thanksgiving fighting the crowds and chasing down the deals. I am not saying that is memory-worthy, but it is the truth. Thanksgiving 2013, however, we threw out tradition and headed to the *Little Cabin on the Trail* in Damascus, Virginia. The *Little Cabin on the Trail* is the place God gave to us after the accident to heal our hearts. I will tell that story later, but for now I want to share how a seemingly ordinary day turned extraordinary.

story time

The cabin, located on the Virginia Creeper Trail (a 34-mile bike trail that was formerly a mountain railroad), is quite cozy. We had spent the previous year renovating it and turning it into our home away from home. It is 600 square feet total with about 300 square feet of area in which to congregate. In the spring, summer, and fall, that is not much of a problem because the great outdoors provides plenty of overflow space. In the winter or when it is raining, it is a bit more challenging, even for those of us who love cozy.

Thirteen people made the two-hour drive north on Black Friday with the intention of eating lunch at the cabin and cutting down our Christmas trees at a nearby farm. It was my sister and her family's first visit. The cabin and its surroundings are truly magical, and I was anxious for her to see the progress we had made. I did not expect her to really experience the full magic of it, however, since it was a bit off season for bikers.

I was totally unprepared for what God had planned.

We knew it would be cold because—well— because we were heading north into the mountains and because—well—because we hadn't quite gotten around to having the heat installed. We did not, however, expect the cabin and the trail to be blanketed in snow, glorious snow. There is absolutely nothing more beautiful than freshly fallen, undisturbed snow in the woods *before* Christmas.

The kids were ecstatic, and my heart did a happy dance inside my chest. Even pre-tragedy, this scene would have thrilled me; but post-tragedy it ministered to me deeply. The tag line on our *Little Cabin on the Trail* sign is *where memories are made and hearts are healed.* I knew that God was healing our hearts once again.

Our group hit the trail quickly, eager to see the transformation the snow had made on our summer and fall playground. The kids served as tour guides as we pointed out to our guests the place we hang our hammocks, the place we search for creek glass, the bridge we walk the dog to each day, and our own Rock City. There were snowball fights, lots of laughter, and, of course, plenty of photo shoots. We even encountered a horse on the trail—in the snow! It was perfect. Some days are like that. Post-tragedy, I do not take those days for granted. I take notice, and I give thanks.

If the story ended here, it would be good enough. The memory of it would still bring a smile to my face, and I would be inclined to remind the children of our first snow at the cabin—at least every year on Black Friday. But it gets better.

Returning to the cabin cold and hungry, I began the task of feeding our small army. I had planned ahead—which is note-worthy—and had a huge pot of corn chowder already simmering on the stove. I started making grilled cheese sandwiches to go along with the soup. To help with the visual, you should know that because the heat had not been installed yet, we were taking the edge off with the oven, an electric heater, and an industrial blower that kind of sounded like an airplane taking off.

People were eating at the table. I mean six people were eating at the four-person table. Three were eating while sitting on the couch, and one was sitting in the comfy chair. I was making the sandwiches, and two other people were helping me pass out the food. There were boots and scarves and mittens and craziness. Just go with me on this. Do you have the picture?

Right smack in the middle of all this lovely chaos, someone knocked at the door. It is not really uncommon for someone to knock on the door of the cabin. According to Internet sources, somewhere between 100,000 and 300,000 people ride the Virginia Creeper Trail each year. That may seem like a big range, but to me it matters not. Whether 100,000 or 300,000, it is still a lot of people without cell phone service in the wilderness. So, just about every time we visit the cabin, someone stops by. They either need an ambulance, a ride to town, a tire pump, a phone, a Band-Aid, or a potty. And sometimes they need something to eat.

That day our guests were hungry; and in their defense, many people have mistaken our fairly large cabin sign for that of a restaurant's and have just walked on in. At least they knocked. I am not sure why with twelve other people *not* cooking, I answered the door. Maybe it is because the cabin is really my domain. I am used to the knocks on the door, and I absolutely love interacting with the people on the trail.

I cheerfully greeted the young girl at the door— after all, I was having a great day. She asked if the cabin was a restaurant because she and her family (mom, dad, and brother) had just ridden the 11 miles down from the top of the mountain, and they were looking for a place to get something to eat. They actually rode bikes down the mountain in the snow?

In all my cheeriness, I told her that the cabin was not a restaurant, but that she and her family were welcome to join us for soup and sandwiches. Then she said, "Really?" And as if her family could not hear the conversation from where they were standing about ten feet away, she repeated the invitation.

The mom then said, "Really?" They all exchanged glances, and then she offered to pay for some food. They must have been famished. Of course, my cheeriness was definitely encouraging them to throw caution to the wind—or at least to the creek. Why shouldn't they just lay down their snow-covered bikes and enter a cabin in the middle of nowhere and eat with thirteen people they had never seen before?

And they did just that. I told you: The place is magical!

I scurried four people away from the table to make room for our guests. I think my son, the police officer, thought I had lost my mind. He had not spent much time at the cabin. There are different rules there. Hospitality is king. And my sister and niece, who would normally err on the side of practicality and logistics, immediately got caught up in the whole experience, making my new friends feel right at home. My husband and daughters had already been smitten with the cabin magic, so they did not even flinch.

I served our guests soup and took their orders for mozzarella or pepper jack sandwiches. We began chatting. It came so easily. It was a divine appointment to take our ordinary day and add the extra. We were given the opportunity to show some bikers the love of Christ, and we seized it—you know, carpe diem and all that stuff—re-affirming what I already knew: God's anointing is on that cabin.

They were from Germany, residing in North Carolina. I am of German descent. Their daughter was a junior. My daughter was a junior. They loved the snow. We loved the snow. Back and forth the conversation went with a soothing rhythm. The daughter asked for seconds, and the mom said that it was the best soup and sandwich she had ever eaten. She asked how I made the grilled cheese, so I shared my unique technique of taking two slices of bread, buttering them, adding some cheese between them, and toasting them on my George Foreman grill. I told you—magical!

If the meal was not impressive enough, my sister had made cookies that the dad deemed something out of a commercial. My brother, a professional chef, after hearing this story, told me it is a fact that the right atmosphere makes food taste better. I agree, but take note that the right atmosphere does not mean perfect. We were crammed into a rustic cabin with heat challenges, eating on paper plates. The right atmosphere consisted of the willingness to offer hospitality to four cold, hungry bikers. They kept saying that nobody in Germany would ever open their door to complete strangers and serve them a meal. I told them that most people in America would not do it either. Most people don't own magical cabins.

I joke about the cabin being magical; but what I really am saying is that when God gave it to us, I specifically prayed for Him to use it for His purpose, that He would give us opportunities to serve others like people had served us in the days and weeks following our darkest hour. I continue to be amazed at how that plays out each and every time we go there.

As the mom was walking out the door to continue the ride down the mountain, she turned to me and said, "We have taken many vacations and have experienced many things, lots of which we do not even remember; but the memory of today will never be forgotten."

It was just an ordinary day, a snippet of life with some snow, grilled cheese sandwiches, corn chowder, a few bicycles, and some of God's children thrown in. It did not really take that much to make it extraordinary. A few days later, I received an email from the dad. He related how he told the people he worked with about his family's experience. They could not believe it. He said it made him realize how uncomplicated life could be. His signature was followed by M.D., Ph.D., MBA. Wow! The part of me that gets intimidated easily would never have extended the invitation had I known how accomplished he was. It is a good thing he hid his credentials under all that snow gear.

His observation about how uncomplicated life could be has really stuck with me. The more I break down the process of making meaningful memories that result in great storytelling, the more I realize that simpler is better.

Characters

I wish we could sometimes love the characters in real life as we love the characters in romances. There are a great many human souls whom we should accept more kindly, and even appreciate more clearly, if we simply thought of them as people in a story. –G.K. CHESTERSON

Everyone takes his or her life for granted to some extent. If your family always goes to the beach, then you don't really have any frame of reference for the person who has never felt sand between her toes or heard the roar of the ocean. If your family has big get-togethers for the holidays, then you cannot imagine feeling lonely on a holiday. My family takes chances, so we have a hard time imagining life any other way. It took a lot of people telling me that we are weird—well, maybe they used a politer word like interesting, but they really did mean weird—to realize that we are a bit unique—unique in a good way. At least I think it is in a good way.

There are people who are quite content to live neat, predictable lives. Honestly, I feel sorry for them. I don't know why really. If they are happy, why shouldn't I be happy for them? I think that I would be bored with a neat, predictable life and deem it to be equivalent to a form of punishment.

I know somebody who, I think, has a neat, predictable life. She is the nicest person you would ever want to meet with a memory for dates and events that is uncanny. She actually remembers the name of every hotel she has ever stayed in and when she stayed there. I can't even remember the ages of my children. Just today when someone asked me the age of my youngest son, I answered, "I don't know. I think he is around 25 or so." Seriously, that is sad. My excuse is that my brain is just so overcrowded with creative thought, I don't have space to file things that I can look up—like on a birth certificate or something.

In all the years I've known this person, I don't ever remember her sharing an oh-my-goodness-you-won't-believe-what-happened-to-me story. There is actually nothing wrong with that. She is not a risk-taker; she likes to play it safe. Somewhere along the line, I am sure she was told some horrible story about what happens to people who do risky things. There isn't much fodder for a good story though with that kind of a life. I believe engaging stories that insist on being told—and not just once—are many times the result of risk taking. I took a risk inviting those bikers to share a meal with us, but I think it paid off in a big way.

I also believe that having an interesting story to tell and developing the skill of storytelling is supported by Scripture. Stories have lasting value. They entertain, encourage, teach, comfort, and connect us to others. They open up doors. Christ told over 40 stories to get His points across. People love to hear a good story. People respond to a good story.

I am one of those people who obviously enjoys doing the crazy thing that other mature adults would not even consider. I am the grandmother that encourages the grandkids and their friends to slide down the banister. I like to fly by the seat of my pants and inject humor in all situations, which is not always appropriate. I strike up conversations with strangers, even ones that do not knock on my door, which sometimes embarrasses my children and grandchildren. I actually crave laughter and "the story" which forces me to sometimes take those enormous risks.

story time

Several years ago, my family hosted a German exchange student named Katja. To be honest, I would not have volunteered to host an exchange student from anywhere; but when my boss flattered me with his high opinion of my family and his belief that we would be a "great" example of a "normal" American family, I relented, all the while knowing deep inside that we are just as dysfunctional as the rest.

My daughter, Kelly; her husband, Travis; and their three children (Ross, Nate, and Kenzie at the time of this story; Ross, Kenzie, and Jett now) share a home in the historic district of our town with my husband, Michael; daughter, Tessa; and me. We have separate living quarters, but the door between the two residences is always open. Children, pets, and visitors drift in and out between the spaces pretty much from morning until night. Being centrally located, it makes for a happening place. I knew that Katja would never be lonely. Then again, if she was an introvert, it was possible that the fit would be less than ideal.

Katja arrived late one evening in August, and the thing that we instantly responded to was her laugh. It was loud, and she found everything funny—and it was loud—and it was late. Maybe it was her nerves—and we prayed that it was—but with that laugh, we were pretty certain that she had a sense of humor and that she wasn't an introvert. It seemed like it would be a perfect fit.

Katja was only with us a couple of days when our normal kicked in. My mother, who lived in Ohio, was given only hours to live. It was the same day I was to report for jury duty and my husband was flying in from a mission trip to Brazil. Katja was immersed immediately into life with the Voccolas.

After we buried my mother, I tried to make life as interesting and rich for Katja's six-week stay as possible. We took her camping and boating and, of course, shopping. She perfected her English, and we did not perfect our German. At least according to her we did not. A few weeks into her visit, we had the opportunity to visit my family in Pennsylvania and attend a patriotic rally in Washington, D.C. with over 300,000 other Americans.

My youngest son, Ryan, had recently been deployed to Afghanistan. Just three days after arriving there, his best friend, Justin, stepped on a land mine and lost his leg. He was recovering at Walter Reed Medical Center in D.C., so we planned to visit him at the same time.

The day was hot. I mean really hot. And 300,000 people is a large crowd, so it was not just hot—it was hot and a little bit too cozy. The rally ended, and it was time to make our way to the hospital. We did what tourists do and asked around until somebody who sounded reasonably confident gave us directions. So there we were: husband, son, daughter, Katja, and I. We were each carrying a backpack and a chair that we had brought all the way from Tennessee and braved the Metro with to ensure our comfort at the event. After the rally, many brilliant people abandoned their chairs, but I am more thrifty than brilliant, so we carried ours—onto the bus.

Admittedly, we are not experts at mass transit. It

did seem logical to us, however, that when the voice from who knows where said that the next stop was Walter Reed Medical Center, it was our cue to get off the bus. So we did.

We walked up to the gate to find that on weekends, that particular entrance was not open. No problem, we would just walk on over to another entrance while lugging our backpacks and chairs in the unbearable heat. Do you have any idea how far apart entrances are at Walter Reed Medical Center? Let's just say that after passing our third locked gate, we were all getting a bit cranky. And, of course, I felt responsible since it was my idea. I think the voice on the bus should have said something like, "Walter Reed Medical Center, not the main entrance." We were all primed for what happened next.

This car slowed down and a man yelled to us, "Hey, were you at the rally?" I am sure the chairs gave it away. We told him that we were and wondered why he cared to know that information. Then he asked us where we were headed. We answered that we were trying to get onto the Walter Reed compound. He informed us that we were not even close to the main entrance. No kidding.

I should have mentioned that the man was driving an old Mercedes. My husband has an old Mercedes. What a coincidence. So when he offered to give us a ride to the entrance, we did not even hesitate. My husband jumped into the front passenger seat and started talking shop and left the rest of us to squeeze in the back—four people with four backpacks and four chairs. His trunk did not open. His back windows did not open. His air conditioning was broken. It was an old Mercedes. There were no door handles on the back doors. Once we were in, we were in. Strange thoughts passed through our minds, and our German exchange student said, "Oh, my parents never would have done this." (This seems to be a recurrent theme with our choices in life.) Then she laughed as only she could.

The story does not end here, however. The good Samaritan thought it would be just dandy to take his sweet time and act as our personal tour guide, explaining the historical significance of neighborhood landmarks on the way to the hospital's entrance. When we finally did arrive, the look on the security guard's face when he approached the car for our ID's was priceless. We felt like Chinese contortionists trying to find them. We did eventually get to see Justin that day. Lucky for us, we had our chairs to sit in while we told him of our adventure—a story that made an awkward meeting less so.

When it was time to leave, I knew that we did not have it in us to return the way we had come, so I approached the in-hospital security guard for advice. I did not just ask him the quickest route to the Metro, but went into the whole story of the Metro ride to the rally, the bus ride, the miles and miles we had walked in the heat with our backpacks and chairs, the ride in the Mercedes with no door handles, etc. I was quite animated. I am a storyteller.

It may have been the confused look on my face as

the guard and his companion tried to explain the shortest route or maybe it was just plain compassion for a worn-out family who had traveled from Tennessee to offer prayers and encouragement to a wounded soldier, but somehow we ended up being transported to the nearest metro station in a brand new, air-conditioned shuttle bus. You see, the shuttle bus driver was hanging out with the security guard. I am pretty sure that "officially" he wasn't supposed to use the shuttle to personally take one family to a Metro stop. Katja just shook her head and said again with her strong German accent, "Oh, my parents never would have done this." And then we all laughed.

She was correct. I don't think I know anyone else who would have gotten in that Mercedes or engaged with a shuttle bus driver in a way that ended in a ride and with a prayer for his daughter who was having surgery that week. I do know it is a memory that will not be forgotten by my family or a young German exchange student.

You may think that all of my encounters with strangers have been positive. I can assure you that is not the case, but even negative encounters can be gleaned for storytelling potential if you survive the experience and work at spinning the tale. Undoubtedly, this skill is naturally easier to develop once you get in the habit of storytelling as a way of preserving your memories. You need an example of a negative experience, don't you?

story time

One day I was shopping at our local Goodwill store with my two daughters and my grandchildren. We thrift shop a lot; and for the most part, other thrift shoppers are friendly and helpful and willing to bond while experiencing the thrill of the hunt. Now I am not saying that I set out to bond with people at the Goodwill, but if I am in the mood to chat or am looking for a character for my story of the day, then I may strike up a conversation.

So on this day, it was very crowded because everything was half-priced. After maybe an hour or so, my daughter, Kelly, and I knew that we needed to start wrapping it up. The kids were getting tired and would soon be hungry, and I was maybe getting a little irritable because there was this annoying, screaming child who should have been taken home and given a nap or lunch or a pacifier or some Benadryl at least an hour earlier or upon *our* arrival at the Goodwill. I just don't find screaming children in public all that endearing. And sometimes their mothers get on my nerves, too.

Because of the sale, the check-out line was abnormally long. The screaming child and his mother were about three people behind us in line. At this point, I was pretty certain that all of our blood sugar levels were about to plummet, so in an effort to be pro-active instead of re-active, I pulled out a snack for our kids. And in that moment, I had a wave of compassion wash over me. I thought that perhaps the little screaming child would also benefit from a snack, and I really felt that the Holy Spirit was prompting me to offer some crackers to the mom for junior. That was a little out of character for me since I would not normally accept food from a stranger for my child. Well, maybe I would if he had been screaming for an hour.

I still can hardly believe what happened next. The mom contorted her face into all kinds of hateful and put her hands on her hips and began screaming at me with all kinds of attitude, "What??? Do you think I don't feed my child? How dare you accuse me of starving my child. I ought to take you out right here. You think I don't feed my child. I ought to punch you in the face."

A simple, "No, thank you," would have sufficed. I was horrified. Everyone in the line was horrified. What was the Holy Spirit thinking asking me to share my crackers? That woman looked mean. When it was my turn to pay for my treasures, she was still threatening to follow me to my car and take me out—all over a cracker. I have never again offered to share our snacks with a screaming child.

As awful as that experience was and as frightened as I was, once we were safely in our locked car and exiting the parking lot, Kelly and I laughed and laughed about the absurdity of it all. Years later, we are still laughing. She was a character that we most likely will never forget because we like telling the story of when I was almost punched in the face by a fellow thrift shopper.

story time

Probably my all-time favorite story of engaging with a stranger happened almost 20 years ago while vacationing in the Smoky Mountains. The Christy series had recently been filmed near where we were staying in Cade's Cove. We were huge fans, so we worked hard at securing the general direction of the "secret" location from someone at the visitor's center. Of course, they did not call it secret for nothing.

We were about to give up when we saw an elderly lady with a cane (which will have some significance later) walking down the country road. I had my husband stop so that I could ask her if she knew where they had been filming. Her response surprised us: "Sure I do. Here, move over, and I'll show you." She proceeded to get in the back of the car with the kids and began giving us directions. *Who just jumps in a car with total strangers?* No need to answer that. We definitely would never have found it on our own. She really knew them *thar* parts.

At some point we pulled off the road and had to hike into the woods where we encountered a large snake spread out across the path. We city folks all took a few steps back, but not our tour guide. She began beating that snake with her cane. She really knew them *thar* snakes. That snake slithered away, and I did not blame it one little bit.

I was overcome with emotion as we came upon the schoolhouse and the log benches. The scenery was beautiful, and it felt as if we had stepped back in time. After we took many photos, our new friend invited us back to her home where she brought out old photo albums and shared her own tales about living in the Smoky Mountains and memories of her deceased husband, an itinerant pastor. I truly felt that God had ordained that experience and gave us a gift that money could not have bought on that vacation.

I know that we all have been told since early childhood to not talk to strangers, but I think that is the most ridiculous advice we could give or take. Strangers are just people that we have not had the privilege to know yet. I can't guarantee that every person you approach is going to provide you with storytelling material, but eventually one of them will give you a story that you will never forget.

Clever

*Which would you rather be if you had the choice—divinely beautiful or dazzlingly clever or angelically good? —*ANNE SHIRLEY, *ANNE OF GREEN GABLES*

I have read several books that have affirmed my belief that to be successful at writing, you have to be willing to draw from the ordinary instead of sitting around waiting for something clever to hit you. I like that advice on the surface because it is meant to empower me and others to develop the habit of writing regularly, knowing that there is plenty to glean from, even the ordinary. But the more I think about it, the more I realize that clever is my ordinary. Honestly, I'm nothing if I'm not clever.

I say that a lot—usually right after I do something remarkably clever, which is almost every day. I am not exaggerating. I really am clever. It is my one and only true God-given talent. You can't really learn to be clever. You either are born clever or you are not. Just like you are either born with a voice like an angel or you are not. I was not born with a voice like an angel and no amount of wishing that I was or even prayer and fasting is going to change that. So I have learned to be content with clever. Now before you get all depressed that you have not personally been gifted with cleverness, let me assure you that everybody can benefit from the inspiration that naturally oozes from clever people.

I grew up in what was probably a middle-class family, but I felt like we were poor since there was never any excess. My father spent that on beer, cigarettes, and gambling. That kind of life, with its lack of security, can be its own kind of inspiration. My mother was a self-taught, accomplished seamstress who made a lot of my sister's and my clothing. She did alterations and designed custom slipcovers and draperies in order to make ends meet. I learned to sew because the machine was always up, the scrap material was always available, and my mother's inspiration was always oozing because she also was very clever.

Growing up with a resourceful mother who was not afraid to try new things or to pick up a hammer or move the furniture around every week probably gave me the courage to take creative chances. The stuff my mother did doesn't seem out of the ordinary in this day and age, but in the 60's, she was not like the other moms I knew. She painted my grandmother's linoleum floor and then sponged a flower design on it. She made bird cages out of metal coat hangers and filled them with artificial flowers. Everybody wanted one. I did not. Whatever creative thing she came up with evolved in her own imagination, stimulated by what she had available to her at the time. Those were the days long before blogs and Pinterest.

story time

When I was a junior in high school, my mother decided to leave my alcoholic father. We had been living in Connecticut away from extended family for about four years. My brother had just graduated and chose to stay in Connecticut, but my sister and I had to move back home with her to Pittsburgh, Pennsylvania. After a few months of living with relatives, my mother rented a second-floor apartment in an old house in the city. A young woman named Claire lived on the first floor with two preschool children. I liked Claire a lot, and I've finally figured out why.

Located on Route 51 in Pittsburgh is the Red, White, and Blue Thrift Store. It has been there a long time, at least since 1974. I know that because that is when I first went treasure hunting there with Claire. Claire did not call it the Red, White, and Blue Thrift Store though. She called it the Goody Pond, a reflection of her outlook on life. In 1974, I realized that a truly clever person could, by adding a little enthusiasm and determination, make something from practically nothing. Claire did not shop at the Goody Pond because it was the trendy thing to do. She shopped there out of necessity: her kids needed clothes and shoes, and she could not afford to shop at a department store. And when she didn't find exactly what she needed, she found a way to make it work. I once saw her repurpose a man's suit into a little boy's suit. It was impressive.

I think that clever people are optimistic people because challenges push them to their creative limits and beyond, and that truly is a happy place. Claire took the life of a struggling single mom and made it look interesting. It was how she chose to live it and how she chose to engage with others. By sharing her cleverness, Claire was energized, and I was hooked. I knew that I wanted to be like her—not the struggling, single mother part—able to take whatever life had to throw at me and find a way to make it not only work, but work well. I have no idea what ever happened to Claire, but I hope that she was affirmed for her efforts and that her children rose up and called her blessed.

Clever people have the ability to manipulate the ordinary in such a way that it quite often ends up being amazing or at least more memorable than it would be if we did not manipulate it. We derive great pleasure in doing things that other people think are stupid, not practical, or totally beyond the scope of their imaginations. If I know that someone thinks what I am about to do is stupid, it just makes me more determined to do it and then tell them all about it when I do. Believe me when I tell you, I don't spend a lot of time planning to do the things I do the way I do them. Mostly the ideas just pop in my head with absolutely no warning whatsoever, and then I get so caught up in the potential story that will come out of them that I just can't help myself. I guess it is part of my giftedness.

Probably not every idea that pops in my head should be acted upon. I just want to put that out there as already in evidence before I tell the next story.

story time

Somehow the Tooth Fairy can spot a home in which a clever person resides a mile away or at least from a safe flying distance. I know this for a fact because she has never been satisfied with just leaving the dollar and making her exit at my house. Nope, she has to do "special" things like leave notes and a trail of glitter with clues leading to the stash, making the children that reside in my home giddy with delight. One night she took it a bit too far, even for a clever person like me.

Daughter Tessa had deemed the Tooth Fairy her best friend forever and personal pen pal after reading and re-reading and re-reading *The Tooth Fairy Letters* by Karen Ray. Probably lots of kids desire to do the same, but as statistics would show if a study were undertaken, less than one percent of them would ever have enough faith to actually act on that desire and make it happen. That one percent would no doubt live with—a clever parent.

Let's just say there was a sufficient correspondence foundation laid well before the night that the Tooth Fairy hijacked my identity. That foundation naturally raised the level of expectation significantly with every tooth that was presented for exchange. The night in question, Tessa had written her usual lengthy letter to her bff and placed it in her usual spot. Unfortunately, by the time the Tooth Fairy's assistant found it, it was very late, and her clever had already turned in for the night. Relying on her back-up clever—which, by the way, is sketchy at best— she decided to write Tessa an email, forgoing the usual glitter and such.

In all fairness, the email was "special." It came from the Tooth Fairy's personal account: toothfairy-4real. However, the clever assistant had no idea that when she set up the email account, it would trump, for the lack of a more technical term, her personal email address and attach itself to her forever and for always. To this day, I . . . I mean her assistant must sign into her blog as toothfairy4real.

Now that is a story. Of course, it will be years before I can actually share it around the dinner table— you know, with the grandkids still losing teeth and all. I might add that Tessa was not impressed. She actually appeared depressed most of the day, which confirmed my belief that a good old-fashioned handwritten letter is better than an email any day.

A great storyteller needs something to work with, and I assure you it really is incredibly simple to add colorful layers to your tales through imagination, resourcefulness, creativity, and a bit of cleverness.

story time

Recently, I brought my two youngest grandchildren to the *Little Cabin on the Trail* for a few days. And because I purposely do not have many toys at the cabin and allow very little movie watching since my plan is to foster the sense of wonder in each of us, I had to get creative when three-year-old Jett was bugging me to hit the trail before I was ready to go.

My ability to improvise kicked in quickly. After determining that we did not have a ball at the cabin, which, along with a balloon, guarantees to keep Jett busy for the longest amount of time, I proceeded to make, not one, but three balls out of some polka-dotted knee socks that I had in the drawer. After neatly rolling and tucking, I then removed the potatoes from the bike basket by the back door and set up an indoor basketball court in the kitchen. It didn't take long for Kenzie to join the game of polka-dotted sock basketball.

To further challenge the two of them, I took a piece of chalk and drew a shot line on the painted cement floor. That, of course, led to all kinds of chalk drawings on the kitchen floor and to me feeling quite pleased with myself. I could not wait for their mother to call so they could tell her that their grandmother let them chalk all over the floor and play basketball in the kitchen. As a bonus, it also brought a very distant memory back to me of a time when my grandmother let my brother, sister, and me chalk on her living room rug. I remember thinking that it was the funniest thing. I think I felt like we were getting away with something. As a matter of record, I do intend to bring a real ball for Jett to play with on our next visit. I kind of think that he will go looking for the polka-dotted sock balls though.

We all must be purposeful in combating a culture that encourages us to use electronics to entertain or keep our kids busy while we accomplish the myriad of things on our lists. It is so sad to see children's natural curiosities and imaginations being silenced and replaced by all things technological.

Even the experts are now acknowledging the negative effects that the lack of creative play is having on this generation, from intellectual and emotional development to obesity. Those reasons are good enough to roll up a pair of socks and play basketball in your kitchen, but think of the memory-making that is being missed. Think of the stories that may never be told.

Holidays & Traditions

What an enormous magnifier is tradition!
How a thing grows in the human memory
and in the human imagination, when love,
worship, and all that lies in the human heart,
is there to encourage it. —Thomas Carlyle

Making meaningful memories at holiday times seem to be the easiest for families to pull off. Holidays naturally lend themselves to the enjoyment of traditions and family get-togethers. People tend to take the time to do what they know should be done throughout the year, like relaxing and enjoying the company of others. Holidays give folks permission to get off the ride that is making their heads spin and to go sit a spell on the bench with some cotton candy or a candy cane or in our family, some pickles.

story time

I have very few great childhood memories, mainly

because, as I mentioned before, my father was a serious alcoholic. He rarely interacted with my brother, sister, or me in a positive, nurturing way. Well, maybe he *never* interacted in a nurturing way. He traveled a lot as a salesman, and a good portion of the money he made either went to feeding his addiction or to playing the numbers. When he was home, there were fights and a lot of unpleasantness.

But every Christmas Eve, we saw a side of my dad that almost convinced us that he did, in fact, care about us. Yep, once a year, we felt special.

We grew up in Pittsburgh where community ties were strong and relationships grounded in cultural traditions and sports. You knew your neighbors; sheesh, you knew when they had bacon for breakfast. Homes were lined up like teeth on a comb and not much went unnoticed. Front porches were not just for decoration.

I am sure that everyone knew that our father was a drunk and witnessed his meanness toward us; but nobody, in that day and age, would have said a word about it. There was a line that people did not cross. That would be considered being "nebby" as they say in Pittsburgh. Do you know that there is such a thing as Pittsburghese, a language that only makes sense to those who live there? I digress.

Well, on Christmas Eve, my dad would actually pay a Santa Claus to personally come to our house to hand out our presents—so what if payment was a fifth of whiskey. He came. To our house. For us. It was my dad's shining moment and our brief glimpse at the man he could have been—the man he should have been.

One year, the front door was left open, exposing Santa behind the storm door to the neighborhood children. I'm sure that my dad had his reasons for not closing the door. It was Pittsburgh. It was cold. I will never forget going up to receive my gift and looking outside to see my friends on their bellies sneaking a peek at *my* Santa. That was my nanana-boo-boo moment.

When I had children, I knew that I wanted to keep that tradition alive. I bought the Santa suit and beard, and for a few years I bribed a friend—with food, not whiskey—to ho, ho, ho his way into my children's hearts. It just was not the same.

Maybe it was not the same because my children had so many other happy things in their lives. Maybe it was because, having accepted the Lord, our focus turned more to Christ than Santa. Regardless, the tradition died out after just a few seasons. Over the years, I have tried instituting other traditions. Only a few have really taken root. They are, admittedly, a bit odd—even to me.

story time

Probably 20 years ago now, a friend introduced us to the pickle ornament tradition. On Christmas Eve, an ornament resembling a pickle is hidden in the tree by a responsible adult—an adult who will not steer a favored child in the direction of said ornament either through subtle hints, grunts, or exaggerated body language. Hey, the stakes are high. The child who finds it on Christmas morning gets a special gift. Well, it used to be special. Now it is pretty predictable. One year, I forgot to plan for the "special" gift, so I went to the pantry and took out a jar of pickles. It seemed appropriate at the time. That jar of pickles was thrown into a gift bag, and just like that a tradition was established. Every year since, that has been the prize. You would think our kids were competing for a trip to Disney World. No kidding.

One year on camera, my daughter was asked what her favorite holiday tradition was, and she described the hunt for the pickle and the prize in great detail. When the clip was played at her school's Christmas program, people thought we were weird. Kids were shocked to think that my daughter and grandchildren actually valued such a gift as a jar of pickles. I think they felt sorry for them. It really did sound bizarre after hearing the other children's normal traditions, like visiting relatives or going to their church's Christmas pageants.

I agree that the customary traditions are great and anchor holidays nicely, but the traditions that set your family apart from all others are what will be talked about in the years to come—those and the traditions that played out differently than expected.

story time

Every year for 39 years, I have put up a Christmas tree. Yes, I know that is not the least bit remarkable in our culture which, in fact, further proves my point. Out of those 39 trees—most of which were lovely, I'm sure—only one stands out as truly memorable. That would be the one that son Ryan cut down when I sent him into the woods at our new home, the *Little Crooked House*, in the middle of 11 wooded acres the day before Christmas. And that would be because it was of a non-evergreen variety, probably a redbud.

Why he thought that was what I had in mind I have no idea. Seriously? There were no evergreen trees on 11 wooded acres? Having just unpacked the moving truck in the snow, I was in no position to be picky. We stuck that tree in an empty mud bucket, threw on what ornaments we could find, and went to bed hoping that Santa would not be offended. I tell that story to make me feel better about neglecting my obligation—however self-imposed—to establishing "normal" yearly traditions that probably will never be talked about anyway.

story time

One year, probably inspired by my feelings of being overworked and under-appreciated, I decided that instead of the traditional Thanksgiving meal in which I did everything and the guests just showed up and consumed endless plates of caloric goodness, we would take a more group-effort approach. We would have a family progressive dinner. I admit that it was a little out of the box and not so traditional, but how do you think traditions get started anyway? You try something. If you enjoy it, you keep doing it. If you don't enjoy it, you don't.

I had to convince the rest of the family that a progressive Thanksgiving dinner could really be doable and great fun. Whether thoroughly convinced or not, nobody was willing to argue with me, so a progressive dinner it would be. Between us, there were three homes available in the same town, so it was decided—by me—that one family would prepare and host the appetizers, salad, and rolls portion of the dinner. One family would host the main meal with turkey and the fixings, and I would lovingly prepare and host the desserts. The family members visiting from out of state just got to be our guests.

To me, the day would have been great whether it unfolded just as I imagined or not. The fun was in doing something we had never done before. If it was a disaster, my family would still be talking about it—as they are accustomed to doing with all of my so-called disasters, thereby depositing yet another item in their crazy-idea-from-mom memory bank. But as it turned out, the Tennessee weather was perfect, allowing footballs to be thrown on the lawn during the day and a cozy fire in the wood stove to be enjoyed in the evening. Nobody had been stuck with all of the preparations or all of the clean-up.

Each of us was able to creatively decorate for our course, and we all enjoyed visiting leisurely in each home. It was one of my favorite Thanksgivings; and although I wish that it had become a tradition, it was destined to be a one-time experience. And I am okay with that because it still makes me smile when I think about it.

The Thanksgiving after the accident, in contrast, was extremely difficult for our family. We were all still reeling from the experience and missing Nate and Noah terribly. Our immediate family and everyone else who was on the boat that day came to our house for dinner. Fifteen people tried valiantly to hold it together while attempting to appear thankful. The truth of the matter was that we were all just going through the motions, not yet able to find comfort in traditions. This was uncharted territory, and even the small task of placing the name cards around the table became a balancing act of emotions. They were Nate's creations from a few years earlier, hand-lettered and personalized with Pilgrims and Indians made from his fingerprints.

Tears will probably always come to my eyes when I place those name cards, but I will still do it. Every year. That tradition, unique to our family, has become a sacred ritual, a holy moment of giving thanks for the mere survival of the unthinkable.

It is not my intention that you adopt any of the ideas shared in this book. That goes for giving your kids pickles for Christmas or trading out your evergreen tree for a twig. I share my stories to encourage you to place value on your experiences, no matter how seemingly insignificant, in an effort to develop your stories. Even if you feel compelled to try making a meaningful memory in the likeness of one of mine or someone else's, please know that it will most definitely look and feel different.

story time

My brother's family has a birthday tradition that I love. We happened to be visiting his home at the time of his wife's birthday quite a few years ago, so we got to experience this tradition first hand. After dinner, the family crown is placed on the head of the birthday person by the last recipient. The family crown is a poofy, regal looking thing, not the Disney princess kind. With the crown on my sister-in-law's head, the candles were lit and "Happy Birthday" was sung. Then, still with the crown on her head, she opened her cards and presents. Cards that had been received earlier in the week had been set aside until this time. Every card was read and passed around the table. Every gift was opened and examined by all. It was a grand affair, even for the adults. Of course, photos were taken before the crown was put away until the next family birthday.

My grandchildren thought it was such fun and began making plans to dig our regal-looking crown out of the dress-up bin before the next birthday. We have since been pretty consistent with the birthday crown; however, it has not delivered the warm fuzzies like it did at my brother's. I think that we have expected too much from that crown. We have ignored the fact that their tradition also includes a meal cooked by my brother, a professional chef. And that meal is served in a home that radiates warmth and good cheer with or without that crown.

The day before the accident was Nate's birthday. He proudly wore the family crown while he opened his presents, and we unknowingly took what would prove to be his last birthday pictures. Those photos make me cry, as they should. It does seem fitting, however, that our last images of Nate are those of him wearing a crown. The irony is not lost on me.

Although my tendency is to change things up a bit when it comes to holiday traditions, the accident has made me cling to some as a way of keeping Nate's memory alive and his place in the family secured. Placing the name cards at Thanksgiving, the Christmas pickle, and the wearing of the birthday crown are three that will not be abandoned or messed with.

I would encourage you to consider the traditions that set your family apart and any holiday experiences that maybe turned out a bit differently than planned and to embrace and celebrate them. The more you reminisce and talk about them, the more likely the chance of them becoming part of the stories that will end up being told around holiday tables for many years.

Happenstance

Life is worth living as long as there's a laugh in it.
—L.M. MONTGOMERY

I was not raised in a very funny home. As a matter of fact, I can't recall one childhood memory that involves side-splitting laughter. That is disturbing and probably qualifies me for some additional therapy. In contrast, as an adult, I find a lot of things worthy of side-splitting laughter. Too often, I laugh out loud at inappropriate times, which makes me want to use my magic powers to become invisible.

A master storyteller is able to spin just about all of life's experiences in humorous ways. My husband and his brothers are master storytellers who feed off one another, commanding the stage at every family gathering. Whether retelling the story of when the refrigerator was accidentally tipped over or of sneaking into Mrs. Mingrone's yard to eat her fruit, their animated tales reduce even the most serious observer to all manner of undignified laughter. You know, snorting and such. The incidents they verbally reenact are actually only funny because of the spin they put on them. Not all stories need a humorous spin, but that is what most of mine get.

When I homeschooled, the highlight of our studies was when we could actually go out and experience what we had learned. One year that translated into 23 field trips, one of which was to a potato chip factory. Now that is quality education if you ask me. When Tessa started attending a private Christian school in 4th grade, I was determined to not forfeit the experiential learning that she was used to and that her siblings had enjoyed. So after her class read *Misty of Chincoteague*, I began planning a trip to Chincoteague Island, Virginia, to see the wild ponies. Since my daughter, Kelly, and I had babies just 30 months apart—I know, interesting or weird or so Father-of-the-Bride-ish—we spend a lot of time traveling and taking educational field trips together. We decided to expand the trip to include New York City; Boston, Massachusetts; and Old Orchard Beach, Maine. We also would visit relatives in Pennsylvania and Connecticut.

It turned out to be a fabulous vacation that brought history and our studies to life. The trip was information-packed and rich in experience. We found the facts shared on tours so interesting and the history fascinating. Too bad I did not take notes because I don't remember even one tidbit of information that I could wow you with. There are two specific incidents, however, that I do remember in great detail, because they are storytelling-worthy.

story time

At the time of our trip, Kelly had three children: Ross, almost 7; Nate, almost 5; and Kenzie, 2. My younger daughter, Tessa, and her friend, Brooke, were both 9. Kelly and I were the responsible adults traveling with five children under the age of 10. I think that is brave or crazy. I like crazy better.

One of the things that really interested all of us before we went on our trip was the idea of taking a ride on a whaling boat in Boston. Honestly, it was *the* thing that we all were most excited about. I understood that. A boat ride out on the Atlantic Ocean to see whales did sound more exciting than visiting the U.S.S. Constitution or even taking a Duck Tour since nobody really understood what that meant. On this side of the vacation, we probably all would be most excited about a Duck Tour if anyone is actually taking notes before planning a trip to Boston or any other place that offers whale boat excursions. But at the time, with our limited experience, riding a whaling boat sounded like a grand adventure—especially in the company's brochure:

> *Looking for a whale watch that requires less travel time, offers the most comfortable ride available and gives you more time viewing some of the world's most fascinating and magnificent creatures? Look no further! This is Boston's only three-hour whale watch cruise aboard high-speed catamarans. This cruise*

will get you to and from the whales in less time, which allows you more time to watch the whales. And, all trips are narrated by professional researchers from the Whale Center of New England, the region's foremost authority on our whale population.

Yes, yes, yes! That was just what we were looking for! Quick, comfortable, fascinating! Yes! How *lucky* we felt that the cost was included in our Go-Boston Card price. I would highly recommend purchasing a GoBoston Card, again for those who are taking notes.

Our little group of unsuspecting travelers awoke early and excited about what had promised to be the highlight of our trip. When we checked in, the girl informed us how *lucky* we were since the seas had been too choppy the past few days to take the high-speed catamaran out to see the whales. She deemed us *lucky*, a sentiment I have yet to forget.

There was a little nip in the breeze when we first boarded the catamaran, so we chose an inside table on the first floor. It was also easier with the stroller and five children. As we positioned ourselves and our stuff, I mentioned that it would be nice if the windows opened so that those staying inside could enjoy some ocean breeze. Keep that thought in mind for later.

The three oldest children and I went out the door to the front of the boat to experience that ocean breeze; I mean, the frigid wind in our faces as we flew across the ocean. I literally thought my earrings were going to rip out of my ears. I was thankful for the hood on my sweatshirt that I was able to securely fasten under my chin. I was a sight, for sure. We quickly realized that we were not dressed for our high-speed boat ride, but we weren't about to lose our good spots up front where we would have prime viewing of the whales. This whole thought process seems ludicrous now.

At one point, I thought it would be a good idea to check on Kelly and the two youngest children inside. I left Tessa, Brooke, and Ross to protect our prime section of oceanfront real estate along the rail. The trip to the door proved much harder than I expected. I like to think that I have pretty good balance. I have never once landed in anyone's lap on the way to the bathroom on an airplane, even if we hit turbulence. Apparently, altitude helps with balance because I felt like a dirty old man groping everyone in my path on the way to the door. Inside everything seemed to be going fine, so I returned to my spot on the rail.

Moments later, things started to go downhill rather quickly—kind of like at the same speed that the catamaran was traveling. The rocking of the boat must have lulled Nate to sleep because he was sprawled out on a bench at our table. Kelly started to feel sick right about the time an announcement came over the loud speaker stating that if anybody was feeling ill, they were *not* to go into the bathroom; they were to go to the back of the boat. I had no idea of Kelly's dilemma, of course, because I was outside having my face flattened by the wind while trying to keep three children from freezing to death on their way to see a whale.

Brooke then told me that she wasn't feeling well, so I went back inside to find Kelly. By this time, she had made her way to the rear of the boat as instructed. There she stood looking green—really green, hanging onto Kenzie. That meant that Nate was sleeping unattended at the table with all of our stuff. I took Kelly some ginger ale and precariously carried Kenzie back to our table. About this time, Brooke vomited somewhere and reported that she felt better. I felt slightly bad that a nine-year-old had to face that alone on a boat in the middle of the ocean, but what could I do? Shiny silver bags were being handed out free of charge and many, many people were using them. I wished that the music was louder.

Kelly took up her position on the floor outside on the back of the boat with the other sick people. I then realized why the windows did not open and was so thankful. By now, looking at them was enough to make anyone start to gag. It was too windy for the people still hanging on to their prime piece of ocean-front property on the front of the boat to use a little silver bag. And that is all I am going to say about that. Brooke threw up a second time and felt better again. I don't know where—probably not in the bathroom.

Tessa started to feel ill next, and Nate woke up. Then Kenzie fell asleep on my lap. After throwing up twice, Brooke had the chills and was shaking uncontrollably, so I attempted to sit with my legs over her for warmth while still holding Kenzie. I began to guzzle ginger ale.

Not really expecting an answer but maybe hoping to get at least a little sympathy, I asked a member of the crew how I was supposed to take care of five children on a boat that everyone was barfing on. He said that maybe I shouldn't have brought five children on a boat. I swear, if I could have, I would have thrown that idiot overboard. Instead I said that their stupid brochure never once mentioned complimentary shiny silver bags or the possibility of your small children being left unattended while you barfed. I knew exactly what it had said.

Fortunately, once we arrived at our destination, at over an hour into the trip, the boat slowed down and some began to feel a little better. Unfortunately, Kelly was not one of them. She remained on the floor at the back of the boat and took the advice of a pregnant woman who, after attempting to rise to her feet to see a whale, strongly advised against it.

Having lost their spots on the front of the boat, Tessa, Brooke, and Ross resorted to running back and forth as the captain spun the boat around in the direction of the whale sightings. I, personally, did not care a flip about seeing a whale at this point. Surprisingly, Nate did not care either. I did manage to catch a couple glimpses, though, through the yucky stuff on the windows. I have no photos to prove it, however, because of, once again, the yucky stuff on the windows.

The professional researcher from the Whale Center of New England could not contain her excitement at the sight of several whales breaching and thought it necessary to tell us how *lucky* we were to see such a sight, since it happens so infrequently. I could not contain my sarcasm at this point and exclaimed rather loudly, "Yep. *Lucky*. That's what we are. Imagine experiencing this much barf and seeing breaching whales all in one day. *Lucky*. That's what we are. That's what the lady told me when we signed in. It must be true. We should buy a lottery ticket."

It was a much smoother ride on the way back, and most folks slept. I bought the children hot chocolate to warm them. Kelly kept her head in a bag and was probably the last passenger off the ship. As soon as we hit the end of the dock, her resolve waned, and she filled her bag. And then she filled it again. And then we all but dragged her back to the car. She finally rallied the next morning and was almost back to normal by noon. My advice: If you want to see a whale, go visit Shamu at Sea World.

My family and I recently took another boat trip out on the ocean to view the lighthouses of Maine. The weather was pleasant, the scenery was breathtaking, and the history extremely interesting. And that is about all I can say to convince you that you and your family should take this tour if you are ever given a chance. I know, I almost sound disappointed that there is no "story" to tell. And maybe I am.

The whaling boat story was not the only one that we brought back from our days in Boston. It wasn't even our favorite. Our favorite involved an encounter with the police. Police stories are always the best.

story time

After a more enjoyable day in Boston, we decided to eat dinner at a restaurant near Boston Common, the oldest public park in the United States. The children noticed that there was a Barnes & Noble next to the restaurant and asked if we could visit it before returning to the hotel. Since it was early, just a few minutes after six, we agreed that it was a grand idea. After all, we all loved books.

I should mention here that we had been training the boys to be gentlemen the entire trip. One of the skills they had pretty much perfected was opening doors for the ladies. It actually became kind of a competition between Ross and Nate to see who could get to the door first. When we arrived at the door to Barnes & Noble, Nate—the younger and smaller—jumped out in front and opened the door wide for all to enter. It was a pretty big door so we applauded his effort.

Upon entering, we thought it was odd that there were not many lights on, and it did seem strangely quiet. But we are all smitten when it comes to books, so were obviously willing to overlook the strange environmental conditions. The buzzing in the background should have been our first clue that something was amiss. Now, don't think we are totally oblivious to the obvious. The buzzing wasn't a loud, alarming sound. It was just kind of annoying, if you know what I mean.

I think Kelly was the first to mention that perhaps the store was not really open. After all, we didn't see any employees in the dim light. Intent on shopping, I kind of thought it would be rude to just leave without at least browsing a bit and giving the employees a chance to come out from the back or from wherever they were. And if the store was really closed, why was it that four-year-old Nate was able to open that big door?

We eventually faced the reality that the annoying buzz was, in fact, an alarm of some sort, and that the store really wasn't open and that perhaps we should leave—which we did as soon as we collected all of the little children. As we exited through the door we entered, I noticed that the deadbolt lock had been turned, but it had not engaged. I decided to do the store a favor by making sure that it was engaged as we left. Just about that time, the police arrived.

Two uniformed policemen came running around the corner and caught the two women and five children breaking *out* of the Barnes & Noble. I mean, of all the places to supposedly break into, we chose a book store! I'm kind of proud of that fact. After some explaining and the officers writing down my personal information for their report, we talked at length about the Red Sox. Their strong Boston accents really were amusing, and I kind of felt like I was hanging out with two characters from Cheers.

I think I have stories filed away on just about every topic. You probably do, too. Recently, the subject of snakes came up. I have absolutely no idea why and am quite certain I did not initiate it; but when an opportunity presents itself, I cannot resist.

story time

We were living in the *Little Crooked House* and learning all kinds of new things, like how to cohabit with mice peaceably—actually that is totally not possible. Before moving to the country when I was 40 something, I actually had no experience with rodents, unless you count the fact that while living in Florida, I frequented the Magic Kingdom.

Country living changes a person. It does. Just months into our move to the top of the mountain, I was quite surprised to find out that I was able to kill a mouse and feel no remorse. Unfortunately, being inexperienced and all, my first attempt at mousey murder did not go so well. I did end up feeling a teensy weensy bad for using a less-than-perfect method. I can't remember how I caught the mouse in the first place, but I do know that putting it in a jar of water was a mistake. Do you have any idea how long a mouse can swim? Let's just say that it was pitiful to watch.

I learned quickly that country mice are plentiful and extremely brazen. Once while talking on the phone, I watched a mouse run across my kitchen counter, grab a piece of a hotdog out of my frying pan, and scamper away. I kid you not. Another time, I watched a mouse—that had obviously consumed some of the poison-laced food that I had put out in an effort to protect my hotdogs—sit down in front of a cartoon with daughter Tessa and grandson Ross. Again, I kid you not.

Eventually, I figured out where the mice were most likely getting in, and I put an appetizing box of poison pellets right at the door so to speak. It was a small hole in the floor of the kids' closet. A normal person would have sealed off the hole; but I knew that if I did that, the mice would just find another way in. I was engaged in psychological warfare with mice. It was not my finest hour.

This technique actually worked quite well for a long period of time. It worked well until the day I walked into the closet and caught some movement out of the corner of my eye at about waist height. I quickly left the closet as calmly as possible and told my husband that there was a snake in the closet. To which he replied, "I am not going to get it out." To which I echoed, "Well, I am not going to get it out."

I should have patched the hole.

We mutually agreed that this was a job for our

country neighbor, Raymond (pronounced Ryemond). He was known to carry a little gun on his side—yes, in plain sight—that he called his snake charmer. I am not really sure if we were okay with him using that gun in the kids' closet or not, but we called him anyway. He was not home.

Our second choice was to call our other neighbor, Robert. Robert was ex-military with some issues that I could never really put my finger on or give a name to. Perhaps it was better that way. We grew accustomed to the sound of automatic weapons while living on the adjacent mountain. I hoped that Robert was having one of his good days. He agreed to help us out and came wielding a machete. A machete? What on earth did he plan to do with a machete?

I did learn an interesting fact about snakes through this experience. When frightened, snakes emit a smell similar to that of burning rubber. Take my advice and don't frighten a snake. Robert caught that snake. I did not watch. He then brought it outside and skillfully used his machete. I did not watch that either.

My husband fixed that hole quick like.

You've heard the saying, "It could only happen to me." Truer words have never been spoken. I can confidently say that the more you look for the stories in life, the more you will find them and the better you will get at telling them. Yes, it does seem to come naturally to me—probably because I am clever—but that does not mean that you can't start looking. You need to capitalize on your happenstance.

Family Fodder

Each day of our lives we make deposits in the memory banks of our children. —CHARLES R. SWINDOLL

I am actually taking a huge risk with this chapter. Telling stories which exploit your family members for a laugh has the potential to make a get-together a huge success or cause it to end prematurely and in tears. My advice is to learn quickly from your mistakes. Know your audience and do try to gauge the emotional health of your subject before starting a sentence with *remember when*.

Tearjerkers sometimes need to be tabled for years, giving the offended party time to come to grips with life and to develop the ability of being able to laugh at his or her expense. Admittedly, some of the best stories may never be able to be shared in public. I have regrettably come to accept that; therefore, stories about a shotgun being fired in the house, snow in Fort Myers, and a child urinating in a doctor's garbage can will not be included in this book. For the most part, my family consists of good sports with broad boundary lines. My experience has taught me that looking back—like years back—at childhood antics is okay. Telling an embarrassing story in public too soon after the incident is definitely not the wise thing to do. No sense in telling you how I know that.

Now that I have that out of the way, I can confidently tell you that your best source of good storytelling material is your own family because it is never exhausted, and it is the most natural thing for you to talk about. My children and grandchildren love to hear stories about when they were little and the silly things they did. It somehow communicates value and love to them. Please do not underestimate the power of telling a story in which your child or grandchild is the main character, especially ones with humorous twists.

After the accident, we told many funny stories about Nate, probably in an effort to delay the inevitable reality of life without him and his daily dose of humor, and because my therapist told me that there is scientific proof that "A merry heart (laughter) does good, like medicine" (Proverbs 17:22). After several days of hearing about Nate's antics, granddaughter Kenzie said, "Tell a funny story about me, Grandma."

Unfortunately, I could not come up with even one. That was very disturbing to me and to her. Kenzie had been an extremely quiet, somewhat dull child. (I say that with all the love in the world.) She had two older brothers and a baby brother. She was perfectly fine with blending into the background and letting them be the objects of everyone's attention. Until that day. On that day, she wanted to be considered for a lead part. Kenzie wanted to be the focus. She wanted to feel valued and loved as Nate had been. She may have known it in her head, but she needed to feel it in her heart. She needed to feel it through laughter.

We almost lost Kenzie the day of the accident as well. Her mom was able to pull her from the water, even as she was being electrocuted. She was carried by a stranger to one of several ambulances because she was unable to walk, and we were unable to tend to her because of the chaos and trauma that was unfolding around us. At our local hospital, already knowing that Noah had died and Nate was in critical condition, Kenzie looked at me with her big eyes and asked, "Am I going to die, Grandma?" I took her in my arms and reassured her that she was not going to die. She was transferred to a nearby children's hospital where she was treated for electrocution, regained the use of her legs, and made a full recovery.

The day she asked me to tell a funny story about her, I considered what our grieving process would have looked like if we had lost her instead of Nate or in addition to Nate. What would we have said about Kenzie? Yes, we loved her dearly, but what stories would we have been able to tell to buy us the time needed to process and heal? Nate had an unforgettable personality and had accomplished much in his short life. He was hilarious, artistically gifted, and extremely driven for a ten-year-old, having just completed a triathlon. I wonder if, knowing how short his life would be, God had allowed him to squeeze a lot into it—for our sakes, certainly not his.

The accident changed us all. Kenzie received counseling that, I believe, enabled her to cope and eventually, thrive, in spite of her harrowing experience and loss. The once shy, introverted child is now engaging and out-going. I am not saying that all children should receive counseling in order to be engaging and out-going. I am saying that Kenzie desired to come out from the shadows, and we recognized that desire and our part in making it possible for her to do so.

Not long after the accident, Kenzie relayed an incident that happened at school that had us all roaring with laughter. It was a huge moment as we declared it a funny Kenzie story that will be told again and again. She was ecstatic. I'd tell it here, but you would kind of need to know the children involved to appreciate it fully.

I do, however, intend to share some of our most popular family stories—all with my family's permission. Well, I'm pretty sure I got their permission. There are so many, but the following have made the cut.

story time

My oldest daughter, Kelly, was 17 when she finally desired or was pushed to get her driver's license—

quite unlike the boys who had theirs within minutes of turning 16. Believe me when I tell you that having your first baby get a driver's license is a pretty important event. Maybe I was a little too invested in the process, because when the DMV official offered to show Kelly what she missed on the written exam (pre-computer age), I was all over it. Yes, she had already passed, but I needed to know what she had missed—as if it was a reflection of me. Having gone through it three times since, I do realize how silly that was. I will never forget the one question and her answer. She will never forget the one question and her answer. Nobody in our family will ever forget the one question and her answer. I do believe this story has been repeated more than any other in our family.

The question: What do double solid lines mean?
Her answer: No passing, low flying aircraft.

Now in her defense, she probably just skimmed, and did not read past the *No passing* part. Not probably, she did just skim and did not read past the *No passing* part. Regardless, we laughed all the way home, and we are still laughing twenty years later.

story time

Keeping with the driving theme, Tessa, my youngest, recently got her license, right before her 17th birthday. It is a little early to be telling her driving stories, but they are just so good, I cannot resist. I did, for sure and for certain, get her permission. She, by far, is my least sensitive child when it comes to sharing embarrassing moments. Before I tell her stories, I want to present some facts to take into consideration in her defense—however weak they may be.

As a parent, I have repeatedly taken some things for granted when it comes to training my children. I have taken for granted that they had keen observation skills. I have assumed that they were paying attention to life happening around them enough to just know certain things. Imagine my shock when not one, but both of my daughters asked me which pedal was the gas and which was the brake. Both of them! And then imagine my shock turning to horror when Tessa asked it a second time—weeks into her driving lessons. "Remind me again. Which one is the brake?" So there you have it. I admit that I did not actually tell my girls which pedal was which before they asked.

Tessa did manage to pass her driving test. For the record, I did not ask to see her answers. A few weeks into her driving solo, I received an early morning text from her: "Your car is an idiot, and parking is stupid."

To which I replied: "Those adjectives are better used to describe the operator of my very nice car instead of my very nice car."

When she got out of class, she called to tell me what had happened. She said that she had to pull over on the way to school because she could not see out the front window. She had the defroster on, but the windshield would not clear. She had to get out and actually wipe the windshield with her hand.

She had to get out and wipe it with her hand?

I calmly asked her why she didn't just turn the windshield wipers on. To which she said, "Whatever." And then I laughed until it hurt. Apparently, I had not told her that dew, just like rain, has to be removed with windshield wipers. Again, my mistake. I probably should mention that it was Tessa's first day of college as a high schooler, and she was a tad bit nervous about that 7 a.m. class.

story time

Just when I thought Tessa was getting the hang of the driving thing—and I let up on the prayers—I got a frantic phone call from her while I was in the middle of getting my hair done. She told me she had a problem, a situation with the car. I immediately asked her if she was all right. She assured me that she was fine and that nobody was injured, but the car was in a somewhat precarious position.

That day she was driving her father's beloved, albeit quirky, 1979 Mercedes. On her way home from school, she decided to stop at TJ Maxx. After pulling into a parking space, she thought better of the idea and decided to just go home instead. Observing that no one was parked in front of her, she then decided to just pull forward instead of backing out of the space. What she did not remember was that there was a three-foot wide median strip in front of her.

Why upon driving up the first curb she did not brake and back the car off of it, we will never know. The next thing she knew, the Mercedes was straddling the median, and she was panicked. She did not know whether to go forward or back, so she called me. Try as I might, I could not understand what she was telling me. She was not clearly explaining it as I just did. There was no way I could get to her—with the foil in my hair and all—so I called her dad. He was busy on a job, so he called her brother, Ryan. I could tell that Tessa was about to burst into tears, so I downplayed the situation and told her to just go shopping until Ryan got there. I told her things would be fine and that the important thing was that nobody was hurt. It was a car. No big deal—to me at least.

Now Ryan is known for his problem-solving abilities and is trained in the fine art of showing no emotion. He is, after all, a member of the Army's Special Forces. Even he could not keep from laughing as he considered his options on the best way to get the car off the median without damaging it. After careful consideration, he formulated and executed his plan of just completing the drive-over. Before he did that, however, he took a photo and texted it to the rest of us. That photo is priceless! Tessa knows the value of a good story and has shared this one many times, which proves my point about her being the least sensitive family member.

story time

Another example of me assuming that my children had keen observation skills happened when my son, Michael, was in early elementary school. One morning after I had dropped him at school, I returned home to some strange odor in the kitchen. It smelled a lot like something had melted or burned. I sniffed around and at first found nothing. Eventually, I opened the microwave oven and noticed that there was a brown burn mark on the bottom of it. This, too, was in the olden days, before the glass turntable things. It definitely was where the smell was coming from. For the life of me, however, I could not tell what had caused it.

To tell you the rest of the story, I have to admit to buying what was, perhaps, the most ridiculous kitchen gadget ever. It was an electric butter melter that looked kind of like a hand mixer. It was called a Hot Topper. I know that because they are selling on Ebay and considered vintage. There would be no point in trying to defend the purchase. Anyway, the electric butter melter was not working quickly enough for Michael, so he thought he could put it in the microwave oven to speed things up. Evidently, I was in my room getting ready and missed the fireworks display in the kitchen. He panicked and just threw the thing in the garbage and proceeded to get ready for school like nothing had happened. Thank the Lord he did not burn the whole house down.

Naturally, I just assumed that my children knew

that electrical appliances should not be put in a microwave oven. I am totally to blame—again. Michael apparently learned to pay better attention because the Air Force trusted him to work on multi-million-dollar fighter jets, and our local police department trusts him with a gun and a Taser and pepper spray. He is also a licensed contractor who sometimes installs microwave ovens, which makes telling the story of when he didn't have enough sense to not put an electrical appliance in one all that much funnier.

Like the other stories I have shared, it would not be appropriate to share the following if child number three had not actually managed to become a responsible adult. How responsible? you may ask. He's the Special-Forces-responsible adult. So there. Ryan, bless his heart—as they say in the south—pushed me to my limit more times than all of the other three added together. Before he became an annoying teenager, he had been positively delightful. One day I woke up, and my violin-playing, horse-riding, adventure-seeking, and very charming son was gone; and I did not really like his replacement all that much. No, I did not. To say his teenage years were not my finest hour as a parent would be an understatement. I really did not think that I'd ever be able to look back and laugh—mostly because I did not think I would live long enough to do so.

One of the things I have prided myself on—however wrong—in my parenting has been the ability to mean what I say. If I threatened it, you better believe that I was going to follow through with it. Every. Single. Time. This had little to no affect on child number three from about age 11 on. Again and again, he would toss the dice, hoping for a different outcome. He lost vacations, privileges, and even the right to use the washing machine and dryer at one point—all to no avail.

story time

The day after attending a conference for parents of teenagers at our church, I decided to try the speaker's recommended approach to get a teenager to take responsibility for keeping his room neat. He guaranteed it to work. Every. Single. Time. I informed Ryan of the new plan. It was quite simple really. Anything I found in his room not where it belonged would be taken to Goodwill—never to be seen again unless he was so inclined to go and buy it back. Up until now, I mostly just opened up his door which led to the fire escape (our house used to be a school) and tossed it out into the side yard. My thought was that he would eventually get tired of cleaning up the yard and put the stuff away. He never did. You may ask why I kept doing it. Because it made me feel good to throw his things.

This new approach was going to be hard for me because I had paid for most of his stuff; but I was at my wit's end, yet again. No sense dragging this out. I might as well have shared this new plan with the dog. I would have gotten the same results. So, while Ryan was at work, Tessa and I went into his room with a garbage bag and filled it to the top. I had a hard time putting in the shirt that I had just bought him from Aeropostale, but I did—because I said I would. Mostly, though, I did not look at what I was putting in the bag. Grab and stuff was my technique.

Just as soon as we had lugged that bag down the stairs, Ryan showed up for lunch. Lord, have mercy. Tessa and I made small talk and avoided looking at the bag right there in the middle of the kitchen floor. Then, lo and behold, a miracle happened right before my very eyes: one of my children's keen observation skills finally kicked in. Without hesitation, Tessa and I made a dash for the door, dragging the bag behind us. Ryan, trying to remain calm, and once again hoping against hope that I did not mean what I had said, asked me what was in the bag. I asked him what he thought was in the bag as I proceeded to put it in the trunk of the car.

I told Tessa to get in as I raced to the driver's seat and locked the doors. I cracked the window to tell Ryan that I was on my way to Goodwill just as I had promised. He was clearly agitated at this point and told me that I could not do that. *Seriously?* He told me that I could not take his stuff to Goodwill. He tried opening the back of the van. He threatened to stand behind it so I could not leave. I told him that I would run him over if he did not move. He finally took me at my word and moved. Finally. I don't think I would have run him over.

I felt sick as I drove away—I mean sicker than I ever did dishing out a consequence to one of my children. I called my husband because I was actually afraid of what Ryan was going to do next. He was so mad. Tessa and I walked into the Goodwill, hoping we were not followed. A smiling lady asked me if I needed a receipt for our donation. Oh, no, I did not want a receipt. I did not want anyone to know where that bag of stuff came from. I had no idea just how many dirty socks were in there.

Ryan was surprising calm that evening. He said that the thing that upset him most was that every sock he owned was in that bag. I told him that he was welcome to buy new ones.

Today, Ryan is probably my neatest adult child, and he readily admits to having been a real pain. He is the furthest thing from a slacker, having achieved what few others do in the military. I like to think that I, in a weird sort of way, prepared him his Army career. I may even deserve some kind of medal of honor for it. I am sure he is not overly thrilled when he comes home and I introduce him as my over-achieving child who could not manage to make his bed when he lived at home. I don't really care if he is thrilled, however, because I am still not over it.

Having been a parent now for 38 years, I have an endless supply of funny stories. Lest you think that I cannot laugh at myself, there's the one about taking Kelly to her preschool Halloween party a week early—after staying up all night frantically finishing her Raggedy Ann costume. And then there was the time I sprayed Kelly's meticulously braided hair with Lysol instead of hairspray. That's enough about me. How about the time my husband backed over the suitcase he placed behind the car instead of ~~in~~ the trunk? Wondering what happened, he pulled forward, and ran over it again. Upon realizing what he had done, he said, "Who was the idiot that put the suitcase behind the car?" To which I answered, "That would be you, honey." Yes, I love to tell that one.

Fod•der (noun) - 1. readily available material used to supply a heavy demand. 2. someone or something that people talk or write about.

putting it

Simple Things

It is the sweet, simple things of life which are the real ones after all. –LAURA INGALLS WILDER

When I decided to write this book, I put out a survey asking people to tell me what their favorite childhood memories were. I am going to include their responses at the end of this chapter, hoping that you enjoy reading them as much as I did. I was not surprised at all to find that their answers supported my belief that when it is all said and done, the best memories cost next to nothing and usually involve time spent with people we love, doing things that, at the time, do not seem especially remarkable. I know that I keep telling you that.

You may think the trip to Disney World, dance recitals, sporting events, proms, elaborate birthday parties, or any other myriad of things that about pushed you over the edge in the planning will make the cut; but I can almost guarantee you that most of that stuff will not. Let me be clear: I am not against any of those things and have enjoyed them all—

some even multiple times. And I fully expect to enjoy some of them again with my grandchildren. Those kinds of things feel great in the moment; but in my opinion, they are too big, too grand, to file away in the intimate corner of your heart and mind to be pulled out when you need a hug, when you are missing someone so much that it hurts.

It is then, in those moments, that I need the memories of pixie sticks, cinnamon rolls, card shuffling, bingo games, shark teeth, campfires, dress-up, bike rides, porch sitting, fireflies, laughter, books, cuddles, etc. In those moments, I need the memories of the ordinary, not the extraordinary.

story time

A few months before the accident, Nate was scheduled to go on a school field trip. He shared with me how he hoped to be put in the group with Mrs. Triplett, because Mrs. Triplett always bought the kids in her group a treat at the end of a trip. The last group had gotten those huge pixie sticks. You could almost see his mouth watering with just the thought of getting one of those things. I felt terrible, thinking that somehow we had deprived him of such a simple pleasure. My daughter lives on a tight budget and is pretty committed to providing healthy snacks for her kids, so it was not really surprising that a giant pixie stick had never been brought in with the groceries. I determined then and there to one day surprise him with one.

I just happened to be on a field trip with my daughter a few weeks later and spotted a box of them in the gift shop of the attraction. For the life of me, I cannot figure out why huge pixie sticks are considered souvenirs, but I digress—again. I probably showed a bit too much enthusiasm about my purchase of three of them. For the record, I did not buy one for my own daughter which may have me feeling terrible again one day. I will never forget how excited Nate was when I presented him with that plastic tube of pure sugar, and I will never see a pixie stick without seeing that smile—the smile that still melts my heart. I cannot, no matter how hard I try, conjure up one single memory of our time at Disney World or Dollywood that does that.

My younger daughter, Tessa, and I were recently cleaning off a bookshelf and got terribly sidetracked as we started reminiscing about all the books. Soon we were totally lost in our fond memories of the stories: where we were when we read them, how they affected us, who we think would enjoy reading them, and such. Like old friends, they brought our feelings to the surface. Our dusting and rearranging turned into more of a love fest, complete with caressing and swooning. This then turned into a deep sadness as we got to thinking about those we know who have rejected reading as a preferred pastime. Sharing my love of reading and books with my children and grandchildren has been one of my greatest joys.

The summer we took that road trip from Tennessee to Maine, I read *The Tale of Despereaux* to the children. At one point in our journey, we stopped at my sister-in-law's home in Connecticut. Of course, the children were not about to miss our reading time. Immediately after dinner, everyone gathered around the table as Kathy cleaned the kitchen. Soon Kathy was just as spellbound as the children. It was she who begged me to read "just one more chapter." I am so thankful that I had the children all sign and date that book after we read it, and I fully expect them to fight over that copy upon my death. All kidding aside, I do fully expect them to one day read *The Tale of Despereaux* to their children or grandchildren and remember that trip and its adventures. I love how Cornelia Funke puts it in *Inkheart* (another favorite):

> "If you take a book with you on a journey," Mo had said when he put the first one in her box, "an odd thing happens: The book begins collecting your memories. And forever after you have only to open that book to be back where you first read it. It will all come into your mind with the very first words: the sights you saw in that place, what it smelled like, the ice cream you ate while you were reading it . . . yes, books are like flypaper—memories cling to the printed page better than anything else."

Isn't that just the most wonderful thing ever? If you are not the best storyteller, you can hang your memories on someone else's story. It makes me want to go grab a book off the shelf, gather my grandchildren, and start reading.

I did not grow up in a home with books, but I remember walking miles by myself to the public library—and I am not exaggerating—to feed my hunger for the written word. I vividly remember visiting a family that actually owned a collection of Dr. Seuss books and thinking how lucky they were. The children in my family are extremely blessed as they have always been surrounded by a collection of great books. I may have been slack about buying pixie sticks, but I have not been slack in the book-buying department.

If in writing this book, I can convince you the value of only one simple, memory-making pleasure to be intentional about, let it be that of reading to your children and grandchildren and to anyone else who will listen.

Favorite childhood memories from surveys:

Going to visit my grandmother who lived in a tiny cabin in the mountains and the smell of wood smoke outside of her house and stepping out the back door to follow the short, curving, mysterious path to her springhouse, then drinking the very cold, crystal clear, clean water there.

Playing softball and my parents cheering me on.

Summers! We never went on fancy or expensive vacations. That's okay because my best memories are of the fun stuff we did each summer, like miniature golf and going to Carvel afterwards; a drive-in movie in the back of the station wagon in our pj's; an all-day family picnic at a lake with aunts, uncles, and grandparents; spending the day at a nearby mini-amusement park; and lots of time spent in the backyard pool.

Spending time with family—the whole family.

Playing outside at my grandmother's house.

One of my favorite childhood memories is when Mom and Dad would get a new baby calf from a large farm in our little town that needed fed on a bottle. I always loved watching and hearing them suck and nudge the bottle real hard. The smell of the milk and the sticky feeling of the powder on your hands when it got wet while mixing it up is also a favorite part of the experience. I still go to my dad's farm and feed the calves. They are so adorable.

Living in another country with my family.

When my grandparents would come to visit.

Boating with my family.

Sunday dinner at my grandparents' house with the cousins.

The year I found out that Santa Claus wasn't real. You'd think that would be a sad thing. And it was. I was crushed because I knew my parents had no money. And if Santa wasn't real, then we weren't getting presents. My dad was in seminary and made $200 a month working at a local Fred's store. My mom stayed home and homeschooled us. What makes this memory my favorite is that the manager of the Fred's store where my dad worked knew he didn't have money to buy us presents. The day before Christmas Eve, he told my dad to walk through the store and get anything he wanted in the toy aisle. His generosity not only blessed my parents who wouldn't have been able to give us anything for Christmas, but it taught me a lifelong lesson: No matter who lets us down in life, God will never let us down. He always comes through.

Playing with friends outside.

My Mammaw.

Our family had a huge cherry tree in our front yard and a huge apple tree in our side yard. My dad built a simple homemade swing for each tree. I would sing and sing at the top of my lungs, swing until I was motion sick, swing as high as I could, and then jump off. What a blessing to not have had a care in the world. We lived on a 32-acre farm and raised a few animals and a lot of our vegetables. We sold milk to the dairy from our cows and sold eggs to the neighbors from our chickens. I didn't see any other kids from school the entire summer. When I would swing I could look out over our farm (hay fields, vegetable gardens, and the valley where we lived).

Going on a road trip to Michigan with my gramma and grandpa. We stopped at Lincoln's birthplace and also saw the Johnny Appleseed orchard.

Singing to the cows with my sister. We grew up on a farm, and the cows would line up along the fence, and we would put on shows for them. They actually stood there and watched us!

Sitting and singing with my Papaw (who lived with us) in a swing under the pecan trees in our back yard.

Going to see *20,000 Leagues Under the Sea* with my daddy, just the two of us. I was wearing a red print dress my mother had made for me. Dad gave me a red carnation that he had (for some reason). I felt very special.

Watching baseball at Forbes Field.

Simple Things

Going to Block Island.

Three brothers and a little girl sitting on their dad's lap listening to stories and jokes. Laughter was unending.

Riding and helping to train horses.

Saying prayers with my dad.

Building sandcastles at the beach and learning to body surf with my big brother.

Camping with my dad.

Being at Grandma's.

My dog, Ginger, consoling me.

My father cheering me on from the stands when I raced.

Listening to stories on tape to the light of the Christmas tree with my parents and watching the Walton's *The Homecoming* on Christmas Eve with them.

Playing outside all day. That feeling of being "free."

Fishing with my daddy.

I have many favorite childhood memories. Most of them involve visiting my grandparents. Even though they lived in the same city as me, it was always a treat. I remember I loved to get in my grandmother's sewing box and take all her thimbles and put them on my too small fingers. I actually have one of her thimbles and pin cushions today. She would also hide little treasures in her sewing box—like rings from gumball machines—just waiting for me to find them the next time I came.

One of my favorite childhood memories is that on Saturday mornings, my father would get on his hands and knees and growl like a bear and chase us around. We would laugh and scream and run and hide. Once my brother was brave and grabbed the bear (my father), climbed on his back, and rode him around the living room.

School was really a happy place for me. I have lots of happy memories of teachers and of reading great books with them and for class.

Christmas. For a day, the world seemed to stop and everyone was happy.

Spending weekends and holidays with family; grandparents' home at the farm; cousins and staying up to the wee hours of the morning, all of us on one mattress on the floor of the living room of the farm-house; gardening; reaping the huge harvest my grandfather would share with us; playing in the barn; learning to cook with Mamaw Ruth right beside me, sharing all her secrets; making perfect biscuits, cornbread, and pies; eating Mamaw Reva's awesome chocolate cake with seven-minute frosting.

Reading stories to my younger siblings from a set of storybooks that came with our encyclopedia set.

Barrel racing my horse.

Christmases at my Aunt Karen and Uncle Ken's house with lots of good food, presents, family members, laughter, teasing, more food, hugs, and picture-taking.

Looking out our front screen door in the evening, smelling the cherry trees blooming, hearing a dog bark and a child's shout.

Sleepovers with my grandmother.

I was born in October so every year, my entire family would go to Cade's Cove the weekend of my birthday, and the leaves would be at their peak. We would have a picnic and hike a trail; and my favorite thing was we all rode horses from the Cade's Cove horse barn.

Going to church each Sunday with my family.

Taking family vacations to Vermont. Harvey's Farm was a working dairy farm with no TV or radio, just family togetherness.

Lake George.

Arts and crafts at the playground.

It was about an eight-mile bus ride to and from school. We would pass by a bakery on the way home and the bread would smell so good to us kids because it had been a long time since our early lunch. We wouldn't get home until around 4:00. We had a really long driveway; so after the bus let us off, we had a few hills to climb and mud puddles to go around to get to the house. I couldn't wait to see/smell/taste what Mother had made for us for supper each day. I thought she was always the best cook in the whole world.

My mom and dad always made a HUGE deal out of Christmas! We ALWAYS got our tree on December 15, and it was a live tree—no fake trees in our house! As a parent now, I realize just how much it must have cost them and the sacrifices they made for us so we could have a wonderful Christmas, full of memories.

Going to the smorgasbord with my grandparents every Sunday. They would let me do things my parents would not, like filling an entire plate with green onions or spending five minutes at the soda machine mixing flavors.

Playing "tea party" with my mother in front of the fireplace.

Coming out of church one Christmas Eve just after midnight and big beautiful snowflakes were coming down. The flakes in the glow of the street lights were something to see.

Visiting our cousins.

Fourth of July in Pittsburgh.

Teaching my dog new tricks.

Mom at home cooking.

Hiking in the Smokies.

Spending time with cousins sliding down the hill beside my grandparents' cabin in the mud and snow.

Sleepovers with my cousins at my grandparents'.

Sitting on my grandmother's lap while she loved me unconditionally.

My brother teaching me to ride a bike up and down the street as he ran beside me.

Building a tree house with my dad.

Spending time alone with my Mom, going out to eat and shopping.

Snow sledding in the back yard.

My grandparents would always sneak and give me money. Each of them would tell me not to tell the other one. Most of the time it was one dollar or less, but they always made sure to give me something when I was there.

Ice skating.

Getting together with cousins and aunts to make homemade candy and cookies for holidays.

I sure hope that reading these made you remember a favorite childhood memory. They proved to me what I already believed in my heart about the importance of the simple things in life and family—especially grandparents. In another chapter, I will develop this theme even further and give you more opportunities to reminisce.

Extreme Faith

Do one thing everyday that scares you.
—ELEANOR ROOSEVELT

This chapter is about storytelling that is the result of serious risk-taking, not the in-the-moment-take-a-chance kind where not much is at stake. Serious risk-taking is usually preceded by serious prayer and planning as well as some serious nail-biting. It can be compared to the Israelites crossing the Red Sea on dry land. When it is over, you are given the opportunity, and I think, the responsibility to set up some memorial stones for your future generations.

We all need to give testimony of when God came through on our behalf in a big, unexpected way. I believe that this kind of storytelling is highly emotional because it pits you against the odds, common sense, and popular opinion. It can even make you sound totally insane and irresponsible. *You did what? What were you thinking? Do you know what could have happened? Did you really pray about that?* Sounding insane and irresponsible has its rewards. People love to be taken captive by the suspense of a faith story.

I believe that everybody, somewhere along the line, has had to make an oh-my-goodness-I-hope-this-works-out decision—mainly because life demands it from time to time. If we are honest, we all have had to do something that pushed us beyond what we thought we were able—mentally, physically, spiritually, financially, or even emotionally. I, personally, can only maintain the status quo so long before I start craving the exhilaration of a good adventure—an adventure requiring great faith.

My biggies when it comes to stepping out in faith all seem to have one thing in common: home. I was a stay-at-*home* mom most of my 38 years of parenting, *home*schooled for 16 years, *home*-birthed my last child, and tried my hand at *home*steading. Each of these experiences came after a huge internal (and sometimes external) battle. There were practical considerations and social pressures to be dealt with. Not one of them was embarked upon without a direct "word" from the Lord.

Let me just tell you that the Lord has no obligation to let anyone else in on your directives. In His infinite mercy, however, He quite often confirms your call through others (besides your spouse). In doing so, at least one person can speak positively about your faith adventure while assuring the wide-eyed that you have not completely lost your mind. By the way, always pray that the person God sends alongside you is at least somewhat credible in the eyes of your friends and relatives. That will make it just a little less frightening—for them.

Every single choice we make along the way is directional, steering our lives along a path that could just as easily have been another. I have chosen to share one of my family's faith stories that has, probably more than any other, affected each one of us and our destinies—because it literally moved us from one life to another.

story time

The year was 1998—the year my first born would get married and my second born would graduate from high school and my third born would turn ten and my baby would turn two. And it would be the year that the chatter about Y2K would reach my ears. But more importantly, it will forever be the year that God led us out of the wilderness of Florida into the Promised Land of Tennessee. I can't believe I just wrote that. It didn't really look like the Promised Land at the time.

Sometimes the opportunity to be courageous and adventuresome is thrust at you whether you want it or not; and sometimes it is the result of a decision to not walk in fear, but to walk by faith and not by sight. Y2K did not panic us or make us fearful. It gave us the push we needed to chase a dream, make a change, to try something risky, to learn something new. (Okay, in the spirit of full disclosure, it is possible that all those years of watching Cinderella had its affect on me as well. Quite honestly, I was not about to be caught with my coach turning into a pumpkin when the clock struck midnight.) So, like many others, I planned to stash away some supplies and learn a few new skills—which I did and have never regretted even though my coach did not, in fact, turn into a pumpkin.

What really appealed to me at the time was the idea of eliminating debt, living in the country, and simplifying. I was a homeschool mom feasting on books like *Little House in the Big Woods* and *Heidi* and *The Girl of the Limberlost*. I wanted to hike the mountains and grow beans and catch luna moths with my children. I dreamed about leaving the Florida heat and humidity and moving back to where there was snow in the winter and fireflies in the summer and leaves to rake in the fall.

I never liked living in Florida. Terrible circumstances, that I will not write about in this book or probably ever, led us to move there in 1987. And while I know our time there was part of God's plan, I was more than happy to move on when our time was up. In 1998, I felt our time was up. As often is the case, circumstances arose that began to force our hands a bit. My husband, Michael, lost his job and had taken a temporary one installing insulation. In Florida. It was awful. Poor thing. That was all I needed to present my case to move. It did not take much convincing.

Our goal quickly became to put our home on the market and find a piece of acreage that we could pay cash for. We had vacationed in the Tennessee mountains several times, so I began researching land for sale there. I sincerely doubted that we would be able to move there, though, once I saw the prices. On our budget, I narrowed our possibilities down to a few remote locations in West Virginia or Timbuktu or some other God-forsaken area. No offense intended if you live in West Virginia or Timbuktu.

In researching our options, I made friends with other like-minded people on the Internet—this was way before blog world. People used dial-up and got to know each other on message boards with no photos. What folks looked like and how they really lived was left to your imagination. And this is where my homesteading story really begins.

A movie that my family and I had watched over and over until we could practically recite it word for word was *Anne of Green Gables*. If you are familiar with it, then you will really understand how we ended up where we did. (If you are not familiar with the movie, I'd strongly advise you to become so at your earliest convenience.) In the movie, Matthew and Marilla Cuthbert are brother and sister who have never married, and who live together in a charming home, Green Gables, on Prince Edward Island. They are older, proper kind of folks. They end up taking in an orphan girl, Anne, which really has nothing to do with my story. Suffice it to say that Matthew and Marilla are the kind of people you would want to visit if you ever did make it to Prince Edward Island, and they lived in a Pinterest-worthy home.

So I became friendly with (on the homesteading message board) this older couple who just happened to be a brother and sister living together on a mountain in East Tennessee. You can see how I was set up to imagine this couple and their little piece of paradise. Their names were—oh, that's right, they shared a name—you know, trying to stay anonymous and all. Their name was *The Survivors*—which I apparently was willing to overlook. They had moved from Florida to East Tennessee, which was exactly what I wished I could do. They were the board experts on many homesteading topics like gardening, chickens, goats, canning, and heating with wood. I spent many hours sitting at their feet, so to speak, learning how to live off the land, just in case I was ever given the opportunity. The seed that had been planted was being watered and growing nicely.

After sharing our desire and intentions on the homesteading board, an invitation was extended to us by my homesteading mentors, ~~Matthew and Marilla~~ The Survivors, to visit East Tennessee. They assured me that beautiful land was available within our budget. I still can't believe I convinced my husband to actually do it, but just days after our daughter's wedding and the selling of our Florida home, we headed north to meet ~~Matthew and Marilla~~ The Survivors in East Tennessee. I was given their address and their names, Ed and Gail. Matthew, Marilla. Ed, Gail. Whatever.

We hooked up a borrowed 28-foot camper to the back of our Suburban and headed off into the sunset.

We were actually homeless at this point, so the stakes were pretty high. Seventeen years later it sounds more crazy to me than ever. For those of you who care to know, I do believe that I was walking as closely to the Lord as I ever have. He was leading me, and I have my prayer journals to prove it.

Imagine the feeling in my gut as we traveled across the mountain—I mean a real mountain with winding roads with no shoulders and very steep cliffs in which to fall off to your death for sure. Oh, the looks from my husband and sons. Thank goodness Tessa was too young to realize the danger. The only thing that kept me going was the thought of Ed and Gail greeting us with a glass of iced tea and big southern smiles. I imagined their sweeping porch with rocking chairs and potted mums.

Now would be a good time to remind you that this was also way before everyone had cell phones and digital cameras—the olden days. So we pulled up to their house, which had been built right into the side of an East Tennessee mountain. I will not lie, the little bit of faith and hope that I had left after the harrowing drive faltered. I thought for sure that I had missed God. And perhaps I did. Even years later, I wonder if we could not have landed where God had intended without that trip over the mountain. I do know for sure that one of my big regrets in life is not making that moment a Kodak moment. Perhaps I was in shock. There was no big porch—or a place to park for that matter. There was no sweet tea. There was no Matthew and Marilla.

The road was narrow, and there was a river down below, opposite the house. And we were in a Suburban pulling a 28-foot camper. I thought my husband was going to shoot me. Thank the good Lord that we had convictions about guns back then. Ed was an ex-hippie with a pony tail, and let's just say that Gail was . . . his sister. They were convinced that the government was out to get us and had been stockpiling all kinds of stuff. I mean boxes and boxes were stacked to the ceiling. It was pretty obvious that we were not exactly kindred spirits as Anne of Green Gables would say.

Another couple from the homestead board had also met up with us at The Survivors. They were from the Washington, D.C. area—pretty normal folks. The fact that I was not the only crazy person around the dinner table that night was of little comfort. Gail was quite hospitable and had cooked up some venison that I'm sure Ed had procured and spinach that had been picked from their garden. The meal was actually quite tasty in spite of the fact that I was feeling sick to my stomach, having just brought almost my entire family to The Twilight Zone.

As if it could not get any worse, Michael blew out two tires when he tried to turn the camper around in order to park in their front ~~yard~~ road, right smack up against the mountain. And then during the night, our pipes froze. We spent a day looking at land, and the following morning, I begged to return to civilization. I didn't care how cheap the land was on that mountain; I had no intention of living there. We got a room at the Holiday Inn Express, and I cried because we were homeless, and our little girl was married, and it was quite likely that we would soon be living with the newlyweds.

My dear husband said not a word. He didn't dare. He knew that I was in a fragile state and on the verge of a mental breakdown. The next day, we found a campground and a realtor. Her name was Sandra, and I am pretty sure she was sent from God to rescue us.

Sandra lived a daring life, so she understood the quest we were on. She also had faith for the impossible, and she proved it by what she took us to see. Just when all hope seemed lost, we came across an 11-acre piece of property within our budget that actually had a house on it. What we really wanted was the land, but if there was a structure that we could live in *temporarily*, all the better. To say that we were not charmed by the house at the top of the long, steep driveway would be an understatement. We were charmed, however, by the tree adorned in a coat of many colors in the front yard. It was as if each colorful leaf was beckoning us to come, come to the mountains. The pond and old barn were not bad either.

Oh, I almost forgot! In an effort to prepare for this adventure to embark on creating a worthy homestead, while I was busy researching gardening and such, my husband and son flew to the great state of Washington to attend a build-a-log-home workshop—not to be confused with a Build-a-Bear Workshop. If only. The fact that neither one of them had built anything bigger than a bookshelf did not deter them at all. They had caught the adventure bug and were in it to win it. They actually believed that what they learned in that week-long workshop had more than qualified them to build our next home.

We made the deal and returned to Florida where Michael deposited me and our two-year-old on the newlyweds' doorstep. How awkward is that you ask? Very. But we owned the house, and our options were limited. He and our two sons then headed back to Tennessee to begin their first renovation project ever, which, little did we know, laid the foundation for the company that has supported our family for the last 14 years. Amazing really, since the house we had just bought did not even have a foundation or any support worth mentioning.

The specifics: 960 sq. feet, no central heat/air, drop ceilings, four rooms, leaky tin roof, moldy bathroom, crooked everything, built by who knows who in a county without such a thing as building permits.

I was once told, "They don't care if you build a bowling alley on your property. It is, after all, your property." It is how it is done in the East Tennessee ~~Twilight Zone~~ country. Up to this point in my married life, I had only lived in nice *new* homes—in suburbs or cities. I had never owned a canning jar or a shotgun. Looking back, my prior life must not have been that interesting. Enough said. The projects: new walls, new ceilings, new bathroom, new kitchen, new roof, new siding, new everything.

We lived on that property for five years. We celebrated holidays and birthdays and life together in that house. We homeschooled in that house, and I read to Tessa—a lot—in that house as she sat on the swing suspended from the kitchen ceiling. And I painted the OSB floors instead of putting down carpeting because we lived in the country with chickens and goats and horses and dirt—lots of dirt. And every spring, I planted a garden and canned my very own tomatoes.

The best part is that we didn't worry about a thing. We owed nobody, and it felt good. I stenciled *And they all lived together in a little crooked house.* on the wall in the living room to let everyone who visited know that we were well aware of our humble surroundings.

We never did build that log cabin, but I did get to watch my oldest son build his first structure, a two-story garage/apartment. And it was nicer—much nicer—than our house. I was so proud of him. Today he is a licensed contractor. I know that I learned more during those five years than during the previous twenty. God graciously allowed each of us the opportunity to explore areas of interest and passion that prepared us for the next leg of our journey.

We ended up moving from that house after my husband received a "word" from the Lord to purchase what I felt was a ridiculous house in the historic district of a nearby city. I did not actually believe it was a "word" so I insisted that we put out a fleece in the form of listing the *Little Crooked House*—

knowing that nobody was ever in a million years going to buy it. I was shocked when it did, in fact, sell just three days after listing it for asking price (more than two and a half times what we had paid for it), for cash. The people, Jaguar owners from New Jersey, asked if we could be out in 30 days. We could and we were. It still baffles me. Today we live in that "ridiculous" house, a house that prior to our purchasing it had been used as a school.

I have lots and lots of great faith stories, but I only share pieces of them occasionally. Maybe because the retelling requires the reliving, and none of them have come without substantial investment of my emotions. There has been much laughter through each experience, but there has also been much shedding of tears.

I'd encourage you to pull your faith stories out from time to time, not just for your family's sake, but for yours as well.

The Cabin

The mountains are calling and I must go.
—JOHN MUIR

Unfortunately, I cannot write about the cabin without telling the story of how God, in His intimate knowledge of me and my family, prepared a piece of prime memory-making real estate on a remote bike path in Damascus, Virginia, just three months after the accident. I have to tell you how God moved upon the owner's heart (a Christian musician from Charlotte, by the way) to give up the cabin at just the right moment in time, at just the right price. So many events led to his decision that it still astounds me. I have to admit that I don't always feel loved by God, or more accurately, worthy of His love. I don't always feel special, or more accurately, special by the world's standards. I know psychologically that probably goes back to my crazy childhood and my less-than-loving relationship with an alcoholic father, but facts are facts and feelings are feelings. I felt like the favorite child the day I found the cabin, and it has since been set as a memorial stone to remind me of God's great love for me.

Because I have not set out to write a book about grief or even feel qualified to do so, I share the following with some hesitation. It would be impossible to not let such a devastating tragedy invade, to some degree, any of my writing. When something traumatic happens in your life, it adjusts the filter through which everything, from that moment forward, is viewed. So, if you don't want to walk through the valley with me on the way back up to the mountaintop, I will understand. Most days, I wish I could skip it as well.

story time

In October of 2011, my family, my daughter's family, and two other families decided to start a new tradition for fall break: to camp at Beartree in southwest Virginia. We had camped a lot together, but this time would be a bit different. Camping at Beartree is real camping, with no hook-ups or cell phone service. There are, however, bears and raccoons and other critters. It is a beautiful state park—in the wilderness.

The weather that weekend was perfect, and the fall foliage was at its peak. The children and adults settled in, playing games, building fires, riding bikes, and engaging with one another. In other words, we got busy making the kind of memories that last a lifetime. Looking back, even three years later, I still consider that weekend to be one of the best of my life.

On Saturday, the majority of our group was shuttled to the top of the mountain to bike the Virginia Creeper Trail. It was the first time for my younger daughter and three of my grandchildren. They all loved the scenic, downhill ride through the state forest and back country so much that they returned the next day to do it again. You might say that my family's love affair with the trail and the area started that weekend. For me, it was to be the beginning of something much bigger than I could have imagined at the time. A small seed had been planted that was destined to grow a journey.

I had no idea that just nine months later, on the 4th of July, our days of laughter and whimsy would be replaced with profound grief. I had no idea that our world would be shaken so violently that hope and purpose would have to be hunted down with an intensity of new dimension for our very survival. Who could have known that Nate and Noah would be taken from us on that day—a day that had started like so many others—with excitement and anticipation?

And then there was that moment when everything changed, forever. The battle to not succumb to the pain—to not put on the proverbial sackcloth and take a break from life altogether was real. But there were other children to consider and more memories yet to be made. There were many broken hearts that needed to be mended. We all had to believe that there was hope yet to be found.

So we prayed. And when we couldn't pray, others prayed for us and with us. And my family held on for dear life as we navigated waters uncharted and unfamiliar. The loss was so very great and the trauma of the accident so very haunting.

Slowly, glimmers of hope did begin to emerge as we allowed ourselves the luxury of enjoying momentary feelings of peace and even pleasure amidst the pain. Laughter crept in without us noticing from time to time to do her work on our souls. Hard decisions were made by each individual affected by Nate's and Noah's deaths. They were personal, very personal.

Some would seek times of solitude. Some would surround themselves with friends and family. Some would cry a lot. Some would hold it in. Some would want to do new things. Some would want to keep old traditions. When October came around again, the family and friends decided that we would return to Beartree. We would ride the trail again. For Nate. For all of us.

The same four families set up camp, but things were not the same. How could they be? Nate was missing, and the cold, wet weather added no cheer. Our intentions toward healing were thwarted by discouragement and doubt. Perhaps this was a tradition that should have been released.

There is, however, something about the spirit of a small child. It has the uncanny ability to distract even the brokenhearted from his or her discouragement and doubt. We now had two-year-old Jett who embraced the wonder of every moment with an enthusiasm that was a force to be reckoned with, giving the weak in spirit a reason to at least try what once came effortlessly: mere living.

So, on a very different Saturday than the year before, we once again set out for the top of the mountain with what I think were unrealistic expectations—expectations which were totally based on the assurances of the eternal optimist of the group who discounted the cloudy skies. He somehow convinced us that the threatening rain would await our arrival at the bottom and greet us then *and only then*. Unfortunately, as sometimes happens, in its excitement, the rain showed up several hours early and decided to accompany instead of greet.

How nice.

I know that I wished I had not agreed to ride the trail that day. I wished that I had stayed back in my vintage camper to read a book or take a nap. At least I would have been warm and dry. But God had other plans. God had heard my lamenting over not just the loss of two dear boys, but also the loss of our "place" on the water where we had spent years making great memories.

He knew that I wanted another place to be able to do that. No, He knew that I *needed* another place to do that. Even if the others could one day return to the lake—and I prayed that they would—I was fairly certain that it would be too painful for me to ever do so. I did not have the benefit of youthful resilience. So I had begun praying for and imagining a new place of escape from the pressures of our lives. I wanted to have faith to believe that God would re-store a portion of what was taken from my family that day.

And as I came down the trail, on that cold, rainy day in October, I saw her, the *Little Cabin on the Trail*. Of course, that was not her name then. I do believe that my heart skipped a beat—and it was not from the 11-mile exhilarating ride in the rain that it took to get there. CABIN FOR SALE BY OWNER wasn't just a sign about a piece of real estate for sale. It was a sign from God.

My merciful God heard my cry for hope, and He sent it to me that day. That little cabin was "it" and I knew it. God rarely answers my prayers with some-thing as grand as a piece of property; but at that mo-ment in time, I was sinking fast, and He knew that I needed a lifeline. I needed a reason to go on living in the present. He knew that I needed to hear His voice telling me that it was okay to live life again.

One month later, we were the owners of the *Little Cabin on the Trail*, and the process of making her our place began. The renovations became my hus-band's and my distraction from grief and pain. God sent us a job to do to restore our hope, and that job was a huge one. My husband and I had to compro-mise on the renovations. He wanted to go big and add a second story. I wanted to be able to use the cabin by the summer *of the same year*. In the end, we agreed that the inside would be totally gutted and reconfigured, but the outside would remain the same, keeping the charm of its mere 600 square feet.

It has been three years since God showed up in a big way and gave us a cabin. I still have a hard time believing it. I knew then, and I know now—for sure and for certain—that the cabin came with strings attached. It's not clear if I attached them or if God did. Those strings enable us to never take His gift for granted. They require us to remember the prayer of dedication I offered over that little slice of real estate in the Virginia mountains.

My prayer was that God would give my family opportunities to serve others from that cabin. We had been shown such kindness by God's people in the days and weeks following the accident that I knew we had to pay it forward. The opportunities have indeed come—so many, that I have lost count. We consider it a privilege to be able to share with others the love of Christ—a love that we did not fully understand until it saw us through an unthinkable loss.

Nate would have loved the *Little Cabin on the Trail*, and sometimes I feel guilty enjoying it without him. Sometimes I consider what the cabin really cost us, and I am overcome with tremendous sadness—which brings me right back to the feet of Jesus. Again and again I must accept the fact that good things do follow tragedy, but I don't ever have to deem the tragedy worth it. What happened that day will always be horrible; it does not have to be justified. So I accept the pain, and I also accept the good gift of the cabin. I accept the loss, and I also choose to serve others in spite of it.

That truly is a model of the Gospel.

Tullian Tchividjian states in his book, *Glorious Ruin*:

> We cling to our notions of a universe that runs on the instinctual system of punishment and reward, action and consequence, this for that. We desire a world that we can control, where suffering is a problem to be solved and everyone gets what he or she deserves; this is the gravitational pull of Original Sin. Like Job's friends, we prefer the safety of "if-then" conditionality. Suffering, however, often serves as an unwanted reminder that reality does not operate according to our preferences . . . Before we can even begin to grapple with the frustrations and tragedies of life in this world, we must do away with our faithless morality of payback and reward.

Many, many times before the accident I tried to analyze and rationalize scenarios in order to make a tragedy more tolerable—for myself. I attempted to figure out what to do or not to do to protect myself and my family from experiencing something similar. In other words, I tried to assign blame to something I could control. I now realize that while we can make choices, like wearing seat belts or life jackets, which leave us with less regret if an accident does happen, there are no guarantees. Life is unpredictable and totally out of my control.

Tchividjian continues:

> If you have suffered the loss of a family member . . . know that God is not punishing you. He is not waiting for you to do something. You don't have to pull yourself up by your bootstraps and find a way to conquer the odds, be stronger, or transform yourself into some better version of yourself. The pain you feel (whatever the degree) may be a reminder that things are not as they should be, in which case it is appropriate to mourn the gravity of that brokenness.

Again and again, my family was commended for our faith and "testimony" in the face of such a brutal assault, but we were broken to the core. And we knew it. There was no comfort to be found in the compliments. At times the pressure of being a "good" testimony for Christ felt like a crushing weight. Our hearts literally hurt and just breathing exhausted us. So what if it looked like we were "handling" everything well. Was that really an indicator of the depth of our faith? What if we had fallen apart and kicked and screamed? What would people have thought if they saw us when we were alone at night wailing in utter misery?

Our response mattered not to God, because He was in it for the long haul with us. I had to come to grips with another truth from Tchividjian: ". . . explanations are ultimately a substitute for trust . . .

The Lord mercifully put to death Job's final idol—
the idol of explanation."

Instinctively I knew better than to verbalize, *Why
us?* But that did not keep me from trying to come up
with an answer in my head. The only answer I got
was *Why not us?* On whom else would I have wished
this suffering, this pain? I did want to trust God. I
had not realized that it was either/or—explanation or
trust—but when I did, I was relieved to choose trust.

So, I wrestled with God through my walk with
grief, never really questioning the truth of the gospel
for my salvation, but questioning how that truth related to my suffering. And in the end, true freedom
has come because I have released not just the need to
justify or understand the deaths of two young boys,
but also the grip I had on this world.

The more I focus on my heavenly home, the more
I am able to enjoy and appreciate the cabin and the
depth of the gift God gave to us. I do not flippantly
say that the cabin is a little bit of heaven on earth. I
know it is. Before the accident, I didn't really think
much about a physical heaven. I just embraced the
idea that it will be better than here, that it was a place
I should *want* to go. After studying more, I have
come to realize that Isaiah 65:17 can be taken literally. God really is planning "a new heaven and a new
earth." A new earth means just that: a new earth. I
imagine our new earth exactly like the earth we
know, only perfected. So as I walk the trails, I imagine doing it again one day in its perfected state with
Nate by my side.

Words

Almost everybody will listen to you when you tell your own story. –BILLY GRAHAM

About a year before I finished this book, I posted to Facebook that I was near completion—I know, so not true, but I had no idea—and that as a final confirmation of the worthiness of my subject matter, I needed some people to join me in a 31-day memory writing project. I was hoping and praying that at least 10 people would agree to participate. Within minutes, I had 6. Two days later I had 30, and the final count was 45.

What happened next blessed me beyond measure. Our little group bonded over our daily visits to our private page where we shared the good, the bad, the simple, the sad, and the downright hilarious tales of childhood. Each day, I would post just one word in hopes of sparking a memory in my participants. I made it abundantly clear that the project was more about awakening memories than it was about writing. Yes, they had to write on the post, but no one needed to be concerned about grammar or sentence structure. It was all about the stories.

We never completed the project because my husband ended up being hospitalized with a serious heart problem about halfway through, but that was okay. We made it far enough to confirm, beyond a shadow of a doubt, that childhood memories are worth sharing. I also ended up with enough stories to fill this last chapter of my book and then some.

I have chosen a selection of the words and what they inspired me and some of my faithful participants to write.

Bike

Denise: My brother Mike is two years older than I am, and my sister Pat is one year younger. When children are born that closely together, there tends to be a lot of lumping. You know—lumped together for birthday parties, privileges, and sometimes even, punishments. One for all, all for one, and all that jazz. Whether things were fair or not never really came into question.

I am going to guess that I was about four years old when my brother got his first bike. I have no idea where it came from, but I assume my parents purchased it and had to make some sacrifices to do so. I assume that because when my brother, being a typical six-year-old, forgot to put the bike away one day and someone stole it, my father handed down a sentence that, to this day, I think was cruel and unusual.

He would never buy another bike. If we wanted a bike, we would have to buy one for ourselves.

And he meant it. He always meant it. Guilty by reason of sibling association. We were little children, maybe ages three, four, and six.

What's even more cruel and unusual is that my brother has no recollection of this unfortunate incident. I was scarred for life by it, and he does not even remember it—which is probably because he was always in trouble for something. I do not lie.

So, a few years later when Mike received money for his First Communion, he bought a bike. Two years later, after my First Communion, I was not allowed to buy a bike. In the spirit of *fairness*, I had to wait until the next year when my sister made her First Communion so we could both buy our bikes at the same time. That's how that lumping thing worked for the middle child.

So Pat and I bought snazzy, matching pinky-purple bikes. And as was customary in our Catholic neck of the woods, a Saint Christopher medal was attached to the bikes to protect us from having accidents. Apparently, there was no patron saint to protect us from theft, so being a quick learner—from my brother's mistake—I made sure I put my beloved bike in the garage *every single night* without fail.

Karen: The first thought that popped in my mind when I saw the word *bike* was an incident that happened when I was seven years old. The oldest of four, I was accustomed to being in charge. In typical first-born fashion, I called the shots as to what my brood of siblings and I would do for fun. It usually involved some sort of game where I was the chief and they were the Indians, or I was the customer and they were my waiters.

On this particular summer afternoon, the game was for me to put my two-year-old sister on the little red tricycle we often incorporated into our games. I stood on the back and pushed her as fast as I could, trying to beat the boys who ran laughing and squealing alongside us. Little Sis hung on for dear life as I zigged and zagged down the asphalt driveway. Then, disaster. I made a sharp turn and Little Sis, the trike, and I went skidding across the hot black surface.

My sweet toddler sister wailed and screamed as blood poured from her chin. Mom and Dad ran to the scene, shouting, "What happened?" Oh, the guilt that flooded my seven-year-old heart. That feeling—of being responsible for something that caused another person pain. The experience left an impression that has remained with me for more than four decades. To this day, I cannot stand the thought that I have hurt someone.

Sonya: I am not now, nor have I ever been, a riding-bike-and-being-outside kind of girl. I'm more of a stay-inside-and-read-while-everyone-else-is-outside-riding-bikes kind of girl. I do, however, have a movie clip of me riding my bike in the driveway, parking it, and showing off my muscles before I went in the house—presumably to read

Niki: On a hot summer day when I was about ten years old, I was determined to ride my bike faster than the boys in the neighborhood. They had made fun of me long enough. I got on my bicycle, said a prayer, and rode to the top of the hill. I was going to show those boys that I could beat them. I also knew (in my imagination) that Olympic coaches were watching me. They would for sure be impressed with my great biking skills.

I took off as fast as lightning! I was in the lead and just had to make a turn to the finish line when I hit the gravel. My lightning fast bike skills, along with the skin of my left leg, went sliding on the pavement for about 30 feet. I lay there bleeding, embarrassed, but victorious because I beat those boys. My mom almost passed out looking at my wounds on the way to the hospital. Needless to say I did not get a hospital visit from any of those Olympic coaches. I will never forget that great bike ride.

Lanette: I really thought I hit the big time when Mom and Dad got me a basket for the front of my bike. I felt like I was so important as I pretended that I delivered newspapers. I threw them onto porches like city folks did. We always lived in the country, so all my bike rides involved riding in our yard, our basement, or on our carport with my brother.

Kandi: My bike was an escape from responsibility. I lived on a long dirt road that was full of dust, shells, and potholes. It was a perfect road for a girl to ride with a gang of neighborhood boys. Sometimes it can be fun to be the only girl. My favorite neighbor was a boy I loved dearly. Most days after school I would bring him a dill pickle (my favorite) and ask him to ride bikes with me. He was several years older and raced bicycles in the area. He often obliged me and would race up and down the road with me.

He tried for days to teach me how to slide my bike sideways and come to a stop. He would do it and I would try, only to slam into him and his beloved bike time after time. I remember so clearly the time I got it. When the cloud of dust settled from my skid, we both let out a giant cheer! These are some of my fondest memories from my preteen years. He didn't mention to me until after we were married that he never even liked pickles!

Heather: As the firstborn of a large family I was quite frequently entrusted with a larger share of responsibility. We lived in a very small town in Pennsylvania, and it was one of my chores to ride the four or five blocks into town to pick up the mail each day from the post office. Mom would often ask me to also pick up an item or two from the small town grocery that was across the street from the post office.

I had a typical 80s girl bike with the banana seat and big handlebars. It was perfectly functional for that five-block ride, and I loved the ride *to* town because it was all downhill. Pedaling back was rather challenging, though, as I carted the mail in a backpack and groceries on the handlebars. I dreamed about, dropped hints, and all but begged for the ultimate "cool ride," a ten-speed with those thin tires and curly handlebars.

When my mom found one at a garage sale, I was on cloud nine. She was silver with pink stripes. She probably didn't make that particular chore any easier, but I felt like the coolest kid ever.

Shona: I'm sure everyone remembers the movie, *The Christmas Story*, and the famous saying, "You'll shoot your eye out, kid!" Well, my daddy kind of told me the same thing when I was in the 7th grade and asked for a 10-speed bike with the curved handle bars and hand brakes. I begged and pleaded with him. He always said no—until the day he finally said I could buy one with my own money.

My neighbor was getting ready to have a garage sale, and there it was—a 10-speed bike for just $20. So off to my piggy bank I went, but I didn't have enough. I was able to get a loan from my grandmother to cover the rest. I was so proud and happy to have my dream bike, and I was off to prove to my daddy that I could ride that bike.

I rode circles around and around my house, and was doing great until my dad came home and parked his truck in the driveway. I came around the house, intending to go beside the truck, but I was going too fast. I pressed on my pedals to stop, but, of course, they only went backwards in a circle. I gained even more speed, and it was either run into the rose bush to the right or hit Daddy's truck on the left. I tried to squeeze between the two, but I struck my face on the side mirror, scraping the entire left side. I gathered myself up and snuck in the back door to the bathroom to clean myself up without Daddy knowing.

Then I went back outside to practice riding some more. It was starting to get dark as I headed to my neighbor's. I sped through their front yard. The next thing I knew, my bike was going forward and I was flying backwards through the air. I landed with a thud on the ground, knocking the breath out of me.

I lay there stunned, looking up at the clothesline that had been put up earlier for the garage sale. It had caught me right across the neck, leaving a whelp mark resembling a noose. I picked myself up again, retrieved my new bike, and made my way back home to face Daddy.

I walked into the house looking like I had just been hit by a Mack truck with my curly hair a mess, grass stains on my clothes, half of my face scraped off, a noose whelp across my neck, and skinned up elbows. I looked like the villain, Two-Face, from Batman. As I went in to kiss my daddy good night, he looked up from his newspaper, took a sip of his coffee, and said, "You'll never learn, will ya, kid?"

Anticipate

Denise: The thing I looked forward to the most when I was a child was going to school the day after getting new shoes or a new outfit. Getting new shoes or a new outfit was a big deal back in the 60s. It is something that happened maybe two or three times a year, usually coinciding with a birthday, the start of school, or Christmas. And occasionally, it happened when a neighbor delivered a bag of hand-me-downs. I would actually go to bed early in hopes of getting to the next day more quickly.

Sabrina: When I was seven or eight years old, my parents went out of town for two weeks to work a youth camp 1200 miles away. My mom had arranged for my sister and me to stay with four or five families during that time. The plan was to spend a couple nights here and there throughout the fourteen days. It was a genius idea because we never got bored.

The first two nights were spent at my grandparents' house. Both mornings when we woke up, there were small gifts and letters from my parents. When we went to our friend's house for a couple nights, the gifts and letters followed us. Every single morning my parents were away, there would be letters and surprises waiting for us, no matter where we were staying. I was amazed that mom had taken the time to secretly deliver these items to each family before they left. After days four and five, I started to anticipate these letters.

I don't remember what any of the letters said or what any of the gifts were, but I do remember feeling more loved by my parents than ever before.

Deb: I have always been crazy about animals. My

grandpa had bird dogs and horses. He lived in a tiny town in Illinois—the kind of town where kids rode ponies down the street. It was the town of my dreams. As an Army family, our summers were mostly spent moving and visiting grandparents.

I spent the summers of 1967-1969 with my grandparents. I joined all the kids in town on horseback, playing cowboys and Indians in a cornfield and stopping by the Tasty Freeze via pony for a cone. I remember watching the astronauts land on the moon in the den with my grampa. It was exciting, but to be honest, I just wanted my grampa to get up and help me saddle my steed. What can I say, I was 12.

I also loved getting to name all the new pups my grandpa had. Sometimes there were a dozen or more. Pointers tend to look pretty identical, but I could tell each apart and remembered every name.

Lisa W.: Snow! Just thinking about the word brings happiness and joy to me. I remember huge snows growing up. Being able to stay home from school, bundling up, snowball fights, and hot chocolate. I grew up on a dairy farm, so snow meant Daddy would have time to spend with us and just enjoy being able to rest for a moment.

I'll never forget one winter when the snow was so heavy, it downed the power lines. We had a generator in the dairy barn to run the milkers, but it was a camp-out in the basement at the house. We stayed warm using a wood stove that my mom made pancakes on, and we slept on pallets. We would play outside till our faces were numb, come in to warm, and do it all over again. I know it was a struggle for adults going without electricity for days, but for me it was a fabulous winter adventure.

Sonya: When I was about five, I woke up one Easter morning to 12 brightly-colored, hardboiled eggs in a tin tray in the living room. Before this time, there had been no visits from the Easter bunny, so this was a surprise! No anticipation here. But there sure was for every Easter after that! Except, the Easter bunny only made random visits to our house. Some years he came, and others, he didn't.

I guess there is something to the behavior modification technique of random reward, because I *always* anticipated Easter morning in case there was a surprise. I don't remember being terribly disappointed if there was no Easter delivery, but I do remember being thrilled when my anticipation was rewarded! I have dutifully carried on the random reward with my children in the form of the Tooth Fairy. Sometimes she came; sometimes she didn't.

Pretend

Denise: A lot of my memories go back to my Catholic upbringing, which seems a little odd since neither one of my parents went to church with any regularity. Actually, the only thing my dad did do with regularity where church was concerned was to drop the rest of his family off at St. George's on his way to the French Club. The French Club was a place where he could drink with his buddies—on Sundays. He may also have been a bartender there. I am pretty sure he was a bartender there. And he definitely was not French.

My grandmother was a devout Catholic who said her rosary every day and prayed to her favorite saints frequently. I can remember going into her kitchen and seeing the statue of Saint Jude, who is the patron saint of *lost causes*, facing the wall. Apparently, she was not happy with his handling of her lost causes, one being my dad and his lack of church attendance.

My dear grandmother, bless her heart, took every opportunity to encourage us to go to church and to pray and light candles for our dad. She was our example of what a "good" Catholic looked like; and because we loved her, we did at least try to honor her requests.

So every year when Lent rolled around, we were expected—at least by my grandmother—to give up something—besides the mandatory meat on Fridays. Most years we gave up candy like the majority of people—which really was not that challenging since candy was hard for us to come by.

One year, feeling particularly spiritual—for the lack of a better word—I gave up watching *I Dream of Jeannie*. It was to be my greatest childhood sacrifice, made in an effort to please the Lord—and my grandmother.

I Dream of Jeannie was my favorite show. It debuted in September of 1965 when I was eight years old. Jeannie had been shut up in a bottle for some 2,000 years before Captain Tony Nelson, an astronaut, found the bottle and released her. Overjoyed, she promised to serve him forever.

The story appealed to my eight-year-old heart and mind, but that bottle represented everything I wanted in life: my very own cozy place with lots and lots of pillows and shiny things.

The next year, when Halloween rolled around, my mom, an expert seamstress, made an impressive looking *I Dream of Jeannie* outfit for me. I am sure that every kid in the neighborhood was just drooling with jealousy. Wouldn't you have been?

That outfit allowed me to take my pretending to a whole new level. With that outfit on, I believed that I could cross my arms and nod my head and get results—just like Jeannie. I created my own bottle in our backyard on a mound of dirt behind a hedge and pretended it was adorned with all sorts of genie things. I even pretended to get small in order to fit through the ~~hole in the hedge~~ top of the bottle. My bottle was off-limits to everybody except Tony. Tony was pretend, too. (This obsession might be likened to today's *Frozen* craze. I could not LET IT GO.)

In all honesty, I don't think there was much difference in my pretending that I was a genie hanging out with Tony and my grandmother *pretending* to manipulate Saint Jude by making him face the wall. Both required vivid imaginations if you ask me.

I am not proud of the fact that I did not last the 40

days without Jeannie. I tried. I really did. Lord have mercy. And I don't doubt that Saint Jude was required to face the wall on my behalf on more than one occasion. Lord have mercy again.

Emily: One of my favorite pastimes as a child was to pretend I was a school teacher. I would prepare my lessons for the day and line up my favorite dolls and stuffed animals on my blue canopy bed. They were the model class which made teaching so much easier; although, I made sure discipline was lovingly administered if needed.

I wrote math and spelling lessons on my small chalkboard easel and chose my favorite read-alouds in hopes that my class would enjoy them as much as I did! I especially loved checking the correct answers on their papers (which were actually my old worksheets) with my bright red pen. Stickers and smiley faces were given out in abundance. Little did I know that I would one day grow up to be a homeschool teacher.

Sabrina: My granny owned several restaurants throughout my childhood. The largest one served as a huge playground for my cousins and me. Our favorite game when we were all together was something we called *Giants*. We would sneak around hallways, banquet rooms, the industrial kitchen, and the dishwasher room pretending we were invisible. The goal was to not be seen by the giants (adults).

If we made eye contact or were addressed by a giant, we had to sit out for five minutes. We also had a Morse code we created to communicate from the public bathroom wall and the staff kitchen bathroom wall by knocking. Even though my mom and aunts who had to work hard at waitressing, may not have looked forward to going to The Four Seasons, it was the highlight of the cousins' week.

Karen: My mom was a clean freak. If yours was, too, then you know what growing up in a clean freak's home is like. She wasn't one of those OCD types; she just enjoyed having everything in its place. I picked up on those cues early in life.

On Saturday morning, it was clean-your-room time. No big deal. I kind of liked it and got a bit of a rush from seeing the results of my efforts. To make the activity more of a challenge, I would pretend that the president of the United States was coming over for a visit. The president was worthy of the cleanest bedroom a girl could ever present, so I straightened my bookshelves with the spines arranged from tallest to shortest and lined up the shoes in my closet with the toes facing outward. I smoothed every wrinkle from my bed, vacuumed under it, and even ran a dust cloth over the doorknobs to remove any finger-prints—all because the president was coming!

Kelly: I grew up a PK (preacher's kid), so every time there was a wedding in our church, I would sneak back into the sanctuary during the reception. I would walk up the white runner, stand at the front among all the flowers, and imagine a day that I would be the bride. The morning of my own wedding, I arrived at the church—not the one of my childhood—and sat alone in the sanctuary for quite some time. I thought a little, hummed a little, and prepared my heart for my day before I prepared my face and hair, no longer a pretend bride, but a real one. I still love every single wedding I attend.

Kimberly: My best friend and I loved to pretend we were famous movie stars! One summer we collected all our costumes from skating shows (mine) and dance recitals (hers) and put together a program where we danced and sang (well, lip synced) to some of our favorite songs. We called ourselves the Groovy Grapes. Just thinking about it makes me smile! We charged the neighborhood kids a dime to come watch us.

Niki: I used to pretend I was pregnant. I would stick a baby doll inside of my shirt, and yes, I would pretend to give birth. One of my cousins was the delivering doctor. I always had girls and was the best mom in the world. What was I thinking? Is this why I ended up with three girls and four boys?

Mel: My earliest memory of pretending was of my best friend and me getting our big baby dolls and swaddling them to look like real babies, then rocking them on the front lawn, hoping neighbors would stop and comment. We lived in a rural area on a back country road. There were only nine cars that ever drove that road. Seven, if you excluded our parents. I'm pretty sure all seven households knew that those weren't real babies, but they would still stop and oohh and aahh and wave and say, "Take good care of your babies, and don't stay outside too late!"

Shona: Cops and Robbers was always a fun thing to pretend play while riding our bikes. And we would pretend to have a restaurant that featured my famous mud pies! My brothers and my cousin would actually eat them. Bless their hearts.

Lanette: I loved to pretend. My house had a huge living room with no furniture in it, so I played there a lot of the time. I would always pretend that I could sing—trust me, if you have ever heard me, you would know I was pretending. I would pretend to have huge concerts where the walls of that room were the crowds of people that would cheer for me. I would sing loudly and to my heart's content. When I became a teenager, I would pretend to be a rock star and throw my hair all around like the crazies did.

Prank

Kolein: I think I was in 2nd grade. We had moved to a new school district, and I was getting to know several girlfriends. Each of us was sharing stories about our families. As the stories went around the room, each one seemed to be upping the ante. *Oh no,* I thought. *What am I going to say?* My family didn't have anything really special to let them in on. I got nervous. Then it was my turn.

What came out of my mouth shocked me as much as it shocked my new friends. "My dad's underarm hair is so long that he braids it. Really long braids. If you ever come over to my house, you'll notice that he always has a shirt on." I was staring into wide eyes and gaping mouths.

Guess what happened? Next time my girlfriends came over for a sleepover, we were sitting around the table having a snack. My dad was serving me and all my new friends. I had completely forgotten about the story of the braided armpit hair. One of the braver girls spoke up, "Mr. Koroly, is it true that you have long braids under your arms?"

My dad cocked his head, looked over at me—I can only imagine the terror on my face—and replied, "Why, yes. Why do you ask?"

Brave Girl continued, "Can we see it?"

"Oh, no!" my father replied. "I have to keep it covered at all times!"

Later, I apologized to him for making up a story. He just laughed. Over the years, the story had a life of its own, with my dad becoming the chief story-teller whenever he met any of my new friends.

Becca: I hid my oldest sister's shoes one day and lied and said I didn't know who did it! I locked my brother out of the house—a lot! I cut my sister's Barbie dolls' hair—all of them. I hid under my mother's bed to scare her! I glued the pages of several library books together cause I thought that was hilarious!

Liza: Once I put Dawn soap in my brother's grape juice. I don't remember why. He tasted it and gagged. My mom didn't believe him and tasted it, too! She gagged and decided that she must not have rinsed the juice pitcher well enough, and she poured the whole thing down the sink! Boy, I was a stinker!

Lyle: One summer, when I was a teenager, my mom was at a conference for work in Minneapolis. My dad, two brothers, and I packed up our old Winnebago Chieftain and drove the many miles to pick her up and continue our road trip to Montana and Canada. My brother decided our family's German shepherd needed to come along. We all knew Mom would not approve, so to distract her from her anger at the dog's presence, we thought it would be a great idea to tell her that my brother stayed home at a friend's so he wouldn't miss football practice.

I will never forget the look on her face when we told her Adam wasn't with us and then how happy she was when she got to the RV, and he was there. Her joy over my brother being with us really did cause her to be thankful the dog had come along!

Fun

Becca: Fun was waking before dawn to travel, catching fish for breakfast, hiking, biking, running in the river, finding new kids to play with, swimming in the lake, catching salamanders, grilling burgers, watermelon left to chill in the river, telling stories around the campfire, playing games all night, staying up way past my bedtime, seeing wild animals, eating berries in the woods, dancing and singing in the rain, climbing trees, shooting guns, driving a jeep, climbing rocks, picking flowers, and hoping to do it all again the next weekend! Spending time at a little cabin in the woods was—and still is—my earliest memory of nothing but uninhibited fun!

Cold

Lisa B.: Growing up on the shore of Lake Huron, cold was our normal. Being snowed in for extended periods was normal. Building igloos, snow forts, even snow tunnels was normal. My memory of cold, however, has to do with my bed sheets. No matter how warm the house was, the sheets were still ice cold. I always wore a nightgown to bed, and as every girl knows, they ride up! The most dreaded cold feeling in the world to me was crawling into bed and those horrible sheets touching my legs.

Holiday

Connie: We took turns hosting Christmas with our extended family that lived in Bristol, Virginia. This particular Christmas landed on a Sunday, and it was our turn to drive to Bristol. It's not too bad of a drive, but after going to church and then having to travel, we all were very anxious to get the party started!

I will never forget what happened that year. We were so very close to getting off our exit, maybe like five or ten minutes, when this huge muscle man drove by us really fast and made an obscene gesture. Well, my dad raced up and got beside his truck and motioned for him to get off the next exit! I can remember ALL of us being terrified. My daddy is not a very big man.

We got off the exit ramp with the huge muscle man following behind us. We all tried to convince Daddy to go on, but he would not. He had something to say to that young chap. My dad got out, and so did the muscle man! I can't remember what all was said, but I remember the end. The muscle man was pointing down in my sweet daddy's face, and my dad said, "If you point your finger in my face one more time, I will break it off!"

Muscle man proceeded to point again, and my dad reached out to grab his finger as fast as he could! Muscle man backed down. I remember being scared, but then so proud of my daddy for being so brave and standing up for his family in that way. In the end we all pulled off alive, and I think that muscle man might even have felt a little bad for "ruining" our Christmas.

And on that note, we wrap up our trip down memory lane with our project participants. I hope you got a feel for how much fun this was for each one of us. More importantly, I hope that a few of the words sparked some memories for you and got you excited about putting together your own collection. I would strongly suggest that you not consider your mind a reliable filing system. I am here to tell you that it cannot be counted on, so you might consider writing your stories down. Start a notebook and entitle it *Secret Weapons*. You know, that's what our stories are: secret weapons to battle the challenging culture in which we are now living.

Treasure

For where your treasure is,
there your heart will be also.
Matthew 6:21

I told you in chapter one that we would eventually review my credentials for writing this book about the importance of making meaningful memories and telling stories. As it turns out, my credentials aren't all that impressive. I don't have a long list of literary accomplishments or college degrees to even begin to justify my humble attempt at communicating my passion. The only things I had at the onset of this adventure were life experiences, a call from God, and a burning desire to write a book. What I am left with as I finish are a stronger belief in the power of our stories, gratefulness to God, and an unbelievable sense of relief that I can scratch another item off my bucket list.

What I hope and pray you are left with are a be-lief in and a desire to share your own stories and the impression that my family and I are not more interesting or more special than you or yours. You might even be aghast at the audacity I have at considering myself an expert at making memories and telling stories, given my impressive *lack* of credentials. That's okay with me. I am to be applauded, however, for finishing this book—because whether a book is loved or not, every author deserves applause for her dedication to the grueling, heart-wrenching, gnashing-of-teeth, most difficult task ever.

All kidding aside, while everyone may not be called to write a book, I am positively certain that everyone is called to live life and to talk about it, *to make memories and to tell stories.* Tapping into our stories is like mining for hidden treasures. Those treasures have the potential to touch hearts and link generations in unbelievable ways. So, in one last attempt to encourage and challenge you, I will share what I consider to be one of the best stories in my repertoire. It is the embodiment of everything I believe to be true and have tried to communicate.

story time

The summer after we renovated the *Little Cabin on the Trail*, I spent a lot of time there, nudging the tagline, *where memories are made and hearts are healed*, toward truth. That was the summer I met Appalachian Trail hikers, Spectrum and Chef John Wayne.

Tessa, Kenzie, Jett, and I had just returned from creek glass hunting and were having some lunch on the porch when a hiker passed by on her way up the trail. Jett, who was three at the time, had become quite comfortable talking to bikers and hikers. He mostly shouted out an informational ditty about the café being a mile away in order to clear up any confusion about famous chocolate cake being available at our house.

On this particular day, Jett shouted a greeting to the hiker, and she offered him a friendly salutation in return. I turned to see to whom he was talking and asked if she was hiking the 11 miles to the top of the mountain. When she told me that she was actually hiking the Appalachian Trail, I was shocked, intrigued, a little concerned for her, and instantly willing to become invested in her hiking journey.

I invited her in for a visit, and she said, "Really? Are you sure?" Why do people find such an invitation strange? Of course, I was sure! I needed to know why in the world a young girl would want to walk from Georgia to Maine, apparently by herself. I needed to know how long she had been walking, what kind of shoes she was wearing, what she was eating, and what her mother thought of her unique adventure.

I grilled her, which didn't seem to bother her one bit. She had been walking for about five and a half weeks. She was from Louisiana. She was 24 and had never hiked before. She had started with a friend who gave up the hike after just a couple of days and went to the beach. She had just loaded up on ten days worth of food. She had been eating a lot of Ramen noodles. Her pack weighed about 40 pounds. She had ditched her tent and all but two outfits.

She found out that cotton clothing took too long to dry and she should have bought her shoes just one size too big instead of one and a half. She slept in the shelters along the trail where mice crawled over her as she attempted to sleep. She had been chased by a bear. She had been accidentally sprayed with bear mace by another hiker. Hiking cost her about $1.25 a day, and she was going as far as her money would take her. She had enough to get to West Virginia at that point. Her family did not seem to have much of an opinion about what she was doing.

Her real name is Amanda. Her trail name, Spectrum, was given to her by another hiker, as is customary. It means colorful, which I am certain she will always be. She had been traveling with friends she met on the trail: Chef John Wayne, Bach, Nails, Wounded Knee, and Crazy *something or other*.

Chef John Wayne wore an awesome hat and allotted precious space in his backpack for culinary necessities like spices and green peppers. Bach played classical music on his guitarlele and was writing a book about a blind man and his dog on the Appalachian Trail. Crazy was . . . well, *crazy*. Spectrum had veered off the AT onto the Creeper Trail to make up some time and catch up with friends after taking a short break—to get away from Crazy.

I asked her what she needed, what we could do to help her on her amazing journey. I wanted—no, needed—to help her achieve her goal, if just her goal of the day. I felt such admiration for her. She was determined, confident, polite, and somewhat fearless. Spectrum was who God sent that day for us to serve.

She simply asked for a safety pin. Surely, we could do more than give her a safety pin. I was feeling generous: *take a shower, have a popsicle, eat a nectarine, load up on some granola bars. Please, let us serve you.* After some convincing, she did.

We traded all of the above, including a safety pin to break her blisters and some cash to enable her a few more weeks on the trail, for her priceless stories. I think we ended up with the better end of the deal. I really do.

The neat thing about Appalachian Trail hikers is that they are as fascinated by and as interested in the people they meet along the way as the people are about them. When they start the hike, they are well aware of the part that others will play in their journeys. People serve hikers all along the trail. They are called trail angels.

When I was done asking her a gazillion questions, she asked us a few. And as we gave her a ride up the mountain to the next entrance to the AT, we shared about God's love for our family and His provision for healing through the *Little Cabin on the Trail*. When I asked if we could pray for her, she said that we could. After we prayed together, we said goodbye to Spectrum and watched as she walked past the 2"x6" painted white blaze which marked the entrance to the trail and disappeared under the canopy of trees.

The day after our visit with Spectrum, we loaded up the car to go home and were pulling away from the cabin when I noticed another hiker coming up the trail. I turned to Tessa and said, "I have to stop and ask him if he's walking the AT. If he is I want to know his trail name. I promise, it will only take *a minute*." Imagine my surprise when he told us that his name was *Chef John Wayne*. I should have known by the hat. Tessa knew then and there that it was not going to take *a minute*.

I could hardly contain my excitement and blurted out, "*THE* Chef John Wayne?" (As if someone else had hijacked his identity on the trail.) "We know all about you," I continued enthusiastically. He, momentarily, looked skeptical, which quickly turned to what I believe was somewhat impressed that his fame had spread all the way to Hoot Owl Holler. (That really is what the locals call our little neck of the woods, by the way.) I may or may not have read a bit into his expression. It all happened so quickly.

It did not take long for me to get to the part about Spectrum's visit the day before. And just like that, I was turning the car around so that Chef John Wayne could take a shower, wash his clothes, eat some food, and share a few tales of his own.

Chef John Wayne's visit was much different than Spectrum's. Of course, many of their stories shared similarities since they both had been hiking the same portions of the trail at about the same time and sometimes together. His experiences were shared through a more contemplative, philosophical lens. Chef John

Wayne is an observer of all things and was very much in tune with the finer details and nuances of his moments on the trail.

He attempted to share those moments with us in a tangible way through his photos—his art. And we took the time to fully glean from the experience. We even pulled out our field guide in hopes of identifying a moth he had photographed.

In a comfortable exchange, he asked about Tessa's poetry and photographs that hung on the wall. He requested that we play the song, "Live Like That," after noticing the picture of the Sidewalk Prophets and hearing about how the song ministered to us after the accident. He asked and he listened, and then he asked some more and he listened some more. And we did the same.

It's much harder to write a list of facts about him, even though I know I asked him a lot of the same questions I had asked Spectrum. It seems more appropriate to tell his story with broad strokes, the same way I feel he has chosen to live his life.

He prepared for the AT by hiking the coast of Florida: *wise*.

He was attempting to learn how to play guitar while on the hike. Fellow hiker, Bach—who gave him his trail name—was teaching him: *willing*.

His brother is a missionary in China: *prayed for*.

His family was following his travels: *loved*.

He found his already-broken-in boots at a thrift store: *blessed*.

He carried spices in his pack: *interesting*.

His walking sticks were given to him by another hiker: *provided for*.

It was he who accidentally sprayed his fellow hikers with bear mace: *forgiven*.

Chef John Wayne also took us up on the offer to drive him to the next Appalachian Trail entrance. Certain that at least one of his friends was now ahead of him, he had some catching up to do. I made sandwiches for him and for Spectrum, just in case. We gave him the few provisions we had left and then took some photos by the cabin sign. The ride to the trail provided us a little more time to get to know one another. Tessa and Kenzie agreed that they were not disappointed at all that our leaving had been delayed. Meeting Chef John Wayne turned out to be a once-in-a-lifetime opportunity.

So he checked his map, and we marveled at how little one needs to hike in the wilderness. And we took some more photos before we prayed.

For protection.

For revelation.

For God to speak through His creation.

Then we said goodbye to our new friend. We assured him that we would continue to pray for him and follow the rest of his journey on Facebook.

Meeting Spectrum and Chef John Wayne affected us all in a profound way. They thought we were the trail angels, but the truth was that they were. Their courage spoke hope into our spirits. Their quirkiness inspired the creativity in us. Their willingness to receive gave us the opportunity to give. Their interest in our lives affirmed our calling to serve the people on the trail. Maybe what matters most, however, is that their stories have given us stories to tell.

A week later when I returned to the cabin, I opened our guest book. It was just as if Chef John Wayne had come back for a quick visit. I was so moved by what he had written:

> "Everything you need is on the side of the trail." God's unfathomable, unconditional love, grace, and mercy are beyond words. Thank you, Denise, Tessa, Kenzie, and Jett for your hospitality! I was hungry and you fed me. I was thirsty and you gave me something to drink. Dirty and you cleansed me. My heart was heavy and in a cage, and you healed and released me. God bless this cabin!
> —Paul McGowan, Chef John Wayne

"My heart was heavy and in a cage and you healed and released me." That is what our stories can do for others. That is what their stories can do for us. They are priceless treasures—precious gifts—that should be valued and cherished and shared often.

So go and make those memories. Go and tell those stories. Laugh together, cry together, meet new people, take some risks, value the simple, establish some traditions; and by all means, be clever about it.

About the Author

Denise Mahr Voccola has spent her life bravely walking the balance beam between responsible and crazy in her quest to make meaningful, storytelling-worthy memories with her family. Three generations of her family share a historic home in Morristown, Tennessee. She and her two daughters, Kelly and Tessa, also share a blog home, *Fifty Seventy Ninety*.

Much Love & Big Thanks

*Delight yourself in the Lord and He will give
you the desires of your heart.* –P<small>SALM</small> 37:4

God used so many people to breathe life back into the desire of my heart every single time I was willing to let it die. Each positive word of encouragement spoken over me and this project was definitely noticed and appreciated.

To my husband, Michael—you gave me the gifts of time, a cabin, and total support.

To my daughters, Kelly and Tessa—you gave me the gifts of acceptance and love even when I whined, vented, and got frustrated.

To my sons, Michael and Ryan—you gave me the gift of example because you never give up, even when things get hard.

To my grandchildren: Ross, Kenzie, Nate, Jett, and Archer—you gave me the gift of purpose.

To all my family members—you gave me the gift of freedom to tell our stories to the whole world. I did ask you, right?

To my sister, Pat—you gave me the gift of prayer every step of the way.

To my brother, Mike—you gave me the gift of confidence by modeling what it looks like to share your passion with others.

To my fellow writing buddies: Edie@lifeingrace, Meghan, Sonya, Karen, Kolein, Mel, Al—you gave me the gifts of understanding and camaraderie.

To my Memory Project participants—you gave me the gift of your priceless treasures.

To Sara and Hanna from Preciously Paired—you gave me the gift of vision with your cover illustrations.

To Jesus, my Lord and Savior—You gave me the gifts of life, hope, and calling and the grace to face them all.

27954514R00087

Made in the USA
Middletown, DE
26 December 2015